INTRODUCTION to

FOOT
TRAILS

in America

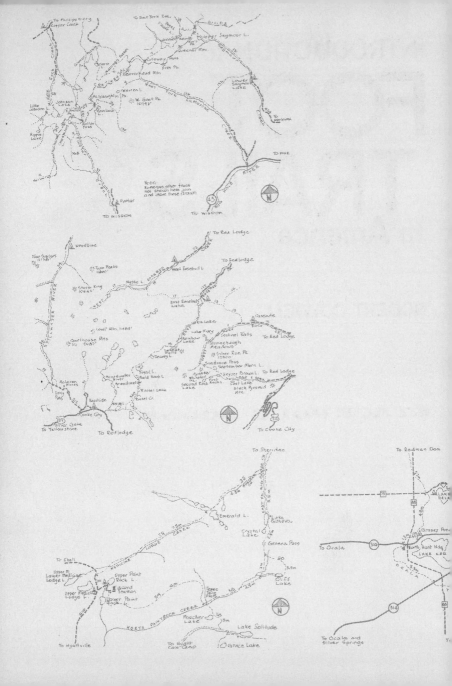

INTRODUCTION to
FOOT
TRAILS
in America

ROBERT COLWELL

STACKPOLE BOOKS

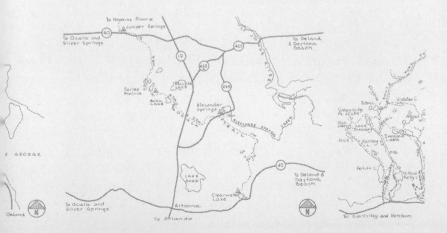

INTRODUCTION TO FOOT TRAILS IN AMERICA

Copyright © 1972 by
Robert Colwell

Published by
STACKPOLE BOOKS
Cameron and Kelker Streets
Harrisburg, Pa. 17105

In order to provide current data this book will be revised periodically.
Please forward to the author, via the publisher, any corrections, addi-
tions, and suggestions.

Printed in U.S.A.

Library of Congress Cataloging in Publication Data

Colwell, Robert.
   Introduction to foot trails in America.

   1. Trails--U. S. 2. Hiking. 3. U. S.
--Description and trails--Guide-books. I. Title.
E158.C76   917.3'04'924   74-179603
ISBN 0-8117-0914-0

To
Roxann and Gary,
who share my dreams

CONTENTS

Urban trails—privately and publicly managed trails near urban population centers

National Trails System—29 National Recreation Trails and longer trails being planned for the future

National and state forests—a variety of climates and environments including mountains, deserts, canyons, prairies, and swamps

The National Park System—30 million acres of excellent hiking country

Wilderness and primitive areas—88 areas comprising more than 14 million acres of the nation's finest wild country

The need filled by this book—a single volume in easy-to-consult format covering selected trails in all parts of America

How to use this book—tips on employing flexibility and imagination to get the most out of this book

Reference maps and guides—best places to obtain them

Touring day hikes—the advantages of this type of hiking in comfort and variety

Chapter 2 Trails East   36

Appalachian Trail—more than 2,000 miles of every kind of hiking from the easy to the arduous

Trails around Washington, D.C.—where to write for information on 45 scenic hikes and the C and O Canal towpath

Trails in Massachusetts and Rhode Island—how to obtain the facts on over 1,000 miles of fine hiking trails in these states

Florida—the lowdown on hiking the Florida Trail, the Ocala Trail, and Everglades National Park

North Carolina—3 2-day trips in Great Smoky Mountains National Park plus tips on hiking in Shining Rock Wilderness, Linville Gorge Wilderness, and Joyce Kilmer Memorial Forest

Kentucky—the outstanding attractions of Cumberland Gap National Historical Park

Virginia—1 3-day and 2 2-day hikes in Shenandoah National Park, within a few hours' driving time for one-third of the U.S. population

West Virginia—5 trips of 1½-2½ days in the Cranberry and Otter Creek backcountries of Monongahela National Forest

Pennsylvania—7 pleasant hikes, from a few hours' to 2 days' duration, on the North Country Trail in Allegheny National Forest, plus notes on the Tan Bark, Susquehannock, Black Forest, Baker, and Loyalsock trails

Chapter 3 Trails Midwest   104

Chapter 4 Trails West   118

Chapter 5 Trails Far West   171

CITY-TRAIL INDEX—
Finding Foot Trails
Near a City

In selecting trails for this book consideration was given to the proximity of urban areas to trail heads. Below each city in the following index are listed those trails and hiking areas within a 125-mile radius, or about 3 hours' driving time, from that city. (In some cases the radius has been stretched.) This index includes over 100 cities, 75 of which have been selected from the 150 cities with populations over 100,000.

AKRON, Ohio
Baker Trail, 80
Black Forest Trail, 79
Buckeye Trail, 107
North Country Trail, 70
Ohio Youth Organizations
    Hiking Trails, 108
Susquehannock Trail, 78
Tan Bark Trail, 78

ALBANY, New York
Adirondack Park, 81
Appalachian Trail, 38
Blue Mountain Lake, 88
Catskill Park, 90
Cranberry Lake, 86
Lake George, 87
Long Trail, 95
Mt. Marcy trails, 83

INTRODUCTION

Few men do not find themselves complete in the wilderness. A day's hike from a trail head brings a welcome transformation. Interests and activities that were of great importance a few hours earlier are subordinated to sensations generated by new sights and smells. The excitement of a wilderness trip pushes aside thoughts of business and home. The satisfaction of accomplishment is given a new dimension, perhaps a fuller meaning, for most of us consider this kind of undertaking a genuine test of our self-reliance. New confidence fills our being as concerns diminish, leaving us with the capacity to savor our new-found solitude and surroundings.

However, a profound change is rapidly taking place in our wilderness. Many of the areas designated as wilderness are actually becoming heavily used and abused. This is to be expected, for these places were set aside to be preserved as singular examples of wilderness. People want to visit them, and are doing so in increasing numbers.

Mount Rainier in Mount Rainier National Park—
National Park Service photo

At present no one knows just how much use a particular wilderness can suffer before irreparable damage is done. Studies are being carried on; controls are being instituted. Quite likely before long there will be a reservation system used in some areas. It will probably be generous. Nevertheless, even though with tight use controls the environment will be protected, the crowds we sought to escape will be found in increasing numbers.

More profound, though, is the loss of the "wilderness feeling" when hiking in many areas. One knows he will soon pass a ranger station, that when he makes camp there will be another half-dozen or more to greet him, that there will be the familiar litter at lakeside, that once wary wildlife will enter his camp as though he were at a busy campground.

People crowd the trails. In keeping with custom they seek the spectacular, the showy, the highest, the deepest, the widest and the most beautiful! Superlatives draw them. It is obvious that under these circumstances one is no longer testing his self-reliance. He is engaged in another form of highly sophisticated recreation—and essentially a team sport at that, for few hike alone.

Aside from this, and more deeply felt by some, is the realization that for most this wilderness experience is not possible. Only a few will make the effort that leads them to a real wilderness where they can test themselves, overcome their fears, and seek that special solitude only found on a remote savannah or mountaintop. It is something not readily known with company. Certainly this value diminishes as the number of companions grows.

Perhaps what is needed is a re-evaluation of what to look for in a wilderness encounter. Rather than spectacular scenery that stimulates and awes, today's hiker might consider searching for quiet in places with less scenic value as measured today. Certainly he would be more alone. The canyons, deserts, and plains of the West offer this kind of environment. So do the swamps and savannahs of the South. The north woods of Minnesota and the lakes of Maine have remote areas seldom visited. The same is true of many mountain ranges in the West.

Despite these observations this book has taken into account the desire of most to visit our nation's natural wonders. This, then, is a book about trails into dense forests cool and fragrant, somber mountain ranges snow-capped above their glaciated valleys, alpine lake country drained by rushing streams, and across sun-hot talus slopes and windswept savannahs.

For many this book will be a starting point. It will help them visit the beautiful and astonishing places written about in the following pages. Some will hike well-traveled routes, while others will seek out remote areas. And surely their wilderness travels will be times of wonder, joy, and spiritual renewal.

CHAPTER 1

TRAILS IN AMERICA

IN AMERICA TODAY there are thousands of miles of foot trails. They can be a narrow, winding, overgrown trace disappearing into the underbrush, or a paved path where people stroll four abreast to view a scenic wonder. These trails follow old animal runways, ancient Indian paths, the routes of trapper-explorers and struggling pioneers. They are utilitarian and recreational; they provide both fire access for forest management and routes leading to fine fishing in alpine lakes.

Trails are a part of our heritage. Their development paralleled our own progress militarily, politically, economically, and socially. They always led to *frontiers*—to the unknown, the new, the better place. Who has not, as a child, come upon a wooded path and either took out to follow it or spent a few moments contemplating its origins, route, and destination. We are a nation of explorers. It is deep in our spirit and customs. Our imaginations are fired by the likes of Boone, Carson, Lewis and Clark.

And more trails are being built. As America grows and leisure time increases, its population seeks respite from itself and turns to the land. Many seek a return to things that were. Others look for their roots in the land. For most it is simply a time of enjoyment in their natural surroundings. Hiking is the means to this end. It is for all those in good health who are energetic, resourceful, and appreciative of the experience and rewards to be had for the effort expended. No one need be an outdoor athlete. It can be a family activity that brings immeasurable gains.

Transportation improvements, better access, equipment advances, and a general mobility of the people makes taking part in this activity easier. As vacationers, we are a nation of travelers; fewer people now than ever hesitate to drive or fly cross-country. This attitude brings the trails of our nation within a three-day drive for most Americans.

URBAN TRAILS

Included in this interest in trail recreation are the programs of trail-building being carried on in many urban population centers like Washington, New York, Philadelphia, Denver, and San Francisco. Managed privately and publicly, these short trails provide for many millions access to historic sites; singular examples of geology, flora, and fauna, and beautiful scenic spots where people can easily visit for a few pleasant hours. Some of them have been designated part of the National Trails System.

NATIONAL TRAILS SYSTEM

Recently inaugurated, this system is the federal government's commitment to improve the quality of leisure and recreation in America. Presently there are 29 National Recreation Trails in the system. Also included in the trail system

Rainbow Falls in Great Smoky Mountains National Park—
National Park Service photo

are the Appalachian and Pacific Crest National Scenic Trails, both of them over 2,000 miles long.

The recreation trails are in or close to urban population centers. They range in length from just under a quarter-mile to 30 miles. On many of these trails hikers must share with bikers and horses. Two trails are used by snowmobiles in winter.

Also under study are several longer trails to be included in the system of scenic trails. The Continental Divide Trail would follow Rocky Mountain summits. The routes of Lewis and Clark, the cattle drives in Texas, and the Mormons, and settlers bound for Oregon are some of those to be considered. In the East the existing Long Trail and proposed North Country Trail will be studied for possible designation as part of this scenic trail system.

NATIONAL AND STATE FORESTS

Many state-owned forests provide excellent facilities for backcountry travel. However, they tend to be small in area, allowing only for trips of short duration. Exceptions to this are regions like the state-administered Adirondack Forest Preserve of New York. Hikers usually turn to the vast federal lands with their wonderful system of trails.

In our National Forest System there are 154 forests and 19 grasslands administered by the Forest Service. These places are located in 41 states and Puerto Rico. Within these forests are found most of our national parks and wilderness-primitive areas. A variety of climates and environments invite the hiker to these preserves: mountains, deserts, canyons, prairies, and swamps.

THE NATIONAL PARK SYSTEM

The 30 million acres of the National Park System provides

excellent hiking country in many of its parks. Most of the trails are well developed and maintained. While some of the parks are small, in some cases a monument or historical site, there are others of great size. Some of the parks most interesting to hikers are described under the various states. Map-brochures may be obtained by writing to the address indicated for each park.

WILDERNESS AND PRIMITIVE AREAS

In America today there are 60 areas designated as Wilderness. Another 28 are titled Primitive, and these are presently under study for inclusion in the National Wilderness Preservation System. These preserves represent more than 14,000,000 acres of the finest wild country in the nation. For information about them write the regional headquarters of the U.S. Department of Agriculture's Forest Service listed under Wilderness and Primitive Areas in the following sections of this book: Trails East, Trails Midwest, Trails West, and Trails Far West.

THE NEED FILLED BY THIS BOOK

Present trail data is copious; yet more trail mileage remains unlogged than has been described. It will probably remain that way for a long time. Many trails are easily followed with no more than signs at trail heads and junctions. This is especially so of trails in the West. Other trails require detailed data, because they are either in barren terrain or heavily wooded areas where the wrong path could be taken. This is evident in places where a lot of logging has been carried on.

There are many fine guidebooks and trail references to be had; some of them are listed in this text. They are all local in nature, providing excellent data about particular areas or trails. For some time there has been a need for a book that covers trails in all parts of our nation. This book fills that need. To be sure, it does not describe every trail in America; such a book would be too cumbersome. Rather, it is a guide to selected trails in easy-to-consult format.

Novice and experienced alike will find these pages worthwhile. New hikers can use them to easily plan their next summer trip or an overnight first. Experienced backpackers, who in the past have restricted their trips to local trails, can with the help of this book check over other trails in search of a possible extended outing away from home. This text will help to familiarize hikers with the trails and area they plan to visit. There will be no need to purchase a number of different guidebooks in order to make a choice. In most cases this book can be used without further references. Nevertheless, supplemental maps, guides, and reference matter will enhance any trip. Names, addresses, and prices of these are included with each trail outline.

HOW TRAILS WERE CHOSEN FOR THIS BOOK

In all, eighty-one trips are described. Choosing trails for inclusion in this book was difficult. Certain criteria were followed in selecting trails. Wilderness status, scenic value, weather, and type of trail were given prime consideration. Variety was also taken into account, but certain areas such as deserts, canyons, and swamps were left out because they are too warm for summer hiking. Some borderline cases are included with the suggestion that they be hiked in spring or fall.

Another consideration was the hiking family or small group. Most of the trails here are suitable for children. Nearly all the trips are loop or return hikes; therefore transportation is not a problem for traveling backpackers.

HOW TRAILS WERE RATED FOR THIS BOOK

Deciding the degree of difficulty or ease of trails is almost impossible. What is arduous for one is quite easy for another. The problem here is one of relative experience and physical condition. Most of the trails in this text were chosen with this in mind. Most can be hiked by novices in good health. Trails considered arduous are noted as so. Generally, six to eight miles can be covered daily in mountain hiking, unless the trail is mostly descending or level. Then ten to twelve miles can be hiked easily.

HOW TO USE THIS BOOK

In the text several recurring headings are used to familiarize the reader with the areas described and to help him, within the scope of this book, to decide on a trip. These headings, and the information they encompass, are as follows:

Season   The best time for hiking and backpacking.

Location   Approximate geographical site.

Access   Generally the most popular or easiest route leading to the area.

Transportation Services   Scheduled bus and air services where they are close enough to be of help.

Accommodations   Location of hotels, motels, resorts and campgrounds in the vicinity.

Medical Assistance   Location of clinics or hospitals, private and public.

Fishing   General note about species, licenses, seasons, etc.

Hunting   As above.

Recreation   Points of interest in the vicinity.

References Other guides, maps, and information that will help make a better trip, and where to obtain them.

Trip Outline(s) Suggested trip outline(s) with sufficient data for taking to the trails.

Observations Further notes on trail data. Trail rating.

In addition to the above information, for most of the suggested trips there is a diagrammatic map showing the trails and route used.

Campsites, as indicated in the text, are only suggestions, although usually based on location of water. There is no reason why camps cannot be made where it suits. Remain flexible and imaginative. Add extra days to any of the trips outlined. Take the time for fishing, photographing, or mountain climbing. Better yet, just sit on a rock and enjoy the surroundings.

Mileages given here are approximations only. Map distances, guide distances, sign distances, and estimates are frequently at odds. Some trail mileages will vary as much as a mile, based on signs at both ends of a trail. Even adjacent signs will vary as much as one-half mile. In some cases hiking time is given rather than mileage.

In this text a trail in good condition is one that is passable. There will be wet spots and rocks to step around, streams to ford and logs to climb over. Remember that a trail in good condition one season can be impassable within a year. Eastern trails become overgrown, while some western trails are snow-covered through July, or obliterated by spring landslides.

REFERENCE MAPS AND GUIDES

Unless very familiar with an area, one should not attempt to hike it without a map. Many maps are prepared by county, state, or federal agencies. Some guides and maps are put together by clubs and organizations whose main interest is hiking and backpacking.

The best maps to use are those prepared by the U.S. Geological Survey. Of interest to the backpacker are the 7½ - and 15-minute quadrangle series. However, these maps do not always have all the trails shown on them. When used in conjunction with a more current guidebook or Forest Service maps, they are quite adequate. Some areas remain unmapped today. Unfortunately many of these areas are the very wildernesses that lure the hiker. Index sheets showing the names and locations of these quandrangles in states west of the Mississippi can be had free of charge by writing:

Distribution Section
Geological Survey
Federal Center
Denver, Colorado 80225

For states east of the Mississippi write,

Distribution Section
Geological Survey
1200 South Eads Street
Arlington, Virginia 22202

When ordering a quadrangle map, be sure to specify name, series, and state in which it is located. List maps alphabetically. Enclose 50 cents for each map.

TAILORING TRIPS TO THE TIME AVAILABLE

When deciding on the length of any hike, most people must keep in mind their limited time—usually vacation time. Two weeks vacation will allow a family from Florida sixteen days to drive to Colorado, backpack in the Flattop Wilderness for six days, perhaps hike two days in Rocky Mountain National Park, and still have time to sightsee the silver mining region around Leadville and Victor. However, most people are weekend backpackers who select trails close to home. For those in the East and West this is possible; in the Midwest there are few trails.

TOURING DAY HIKES

By far the largest number of hikes taken today are of the day variety, though usually in heavily used areas and of short mileage as in interpretive and scenic walks. Not enough notice has been taken of the touring day-hiker traveling to outstanding trail country, extensively hiking the area within the limits set by this method, and then moving on to another region. To be considered this way are longer hikes of from twelve to sixteen miles a day. Without a pack this is a reasonable distance even on difficult trails. Two miles an hour is a comfortable pace.

While it is true that a backcountry feeling cannot always be had this way, countless trails do provide this a mile in from the trail head. Often these will be return hikes, especially in the West. In the East more loop hikes will be found under twenty miles. National and state parks have the most extensive trail systems within their boundaries. It may require several days to exhaust all the possible short hikes in some parks.

Gear for these outings is minimal: a small day pack, raingear, a lunch, and plenty of snacks. Carry a cup. If water must be carried, use a one-quart aluminum bottle wrapped in newspaper; the water will stay cold until lunch. Make sure to include matches and moleskin patches. A compass and maps are essential. For detailed information on equipment, clothing, food, shelter, safety, and all the knowledge needed to insure a safe and comfortable trip of a day or longer, consult *Introduction to Backpacking* by this author.

There are advantages to day hiking. It encourages people to hike alone. One can get a good feeling for an area such as Glacier National Park or the Green Mountains of Vermont. Variety can be stimulating. Returning in the evening to a good meal and a comfortable bed is also a big plus. Moreover, it can fit into the schedules of those active hikers with limited leisure time.

CHAPTER 2

TRAILS EAST

IN THE EASTERN states a variety of wilderness outings can be had by the hiker. The lake country of Maine. The wild and rugged peaks of the White Mountains in New Hampshire. The rolling Alleghenies or the forested slopes of Virginia and North Carolina. The windswept grasslands of Florida in the winter. All of them, sometimes crowded, offer areas of interest to the backpacker.

Generally there is a softness of topography to eastern forest land. Barren peaks are not common. Forest green cloaks most summits. The highest point in the East is North Carolina's Mt. Mitchell at 6,684 feet. Nevertheless, elevation changes on the trail can be great. Hiking is often arduous; few spots in this country offer the challenge of the White Mountains. And the beauty and solitude of Florida's savannahs is unequalled. Spring and fall colors in the Smoky Mountains are matchless.

Half of our nation's population is within a two-day drive of any one of these places. Fine access highways and a vari-

Atop Mt. Washington in the White Mountains of New Hampshire

ety of accommodations will help make a smooth and pleasant trip. Combination hiking-sightseeing vacations are popular in the East, where short hikes are many and historical and recreational points of interest crowd the road maps. A three-day hike in Shenandoah National Park coupled with the investigation of the numerous Civil War sites in the region will make a memorable vacation.

WILDERNESS AND PRIMITIVE AREAS

For information about officially designated wilderness and primitive areas in the East, write the southern and eastern regional headquarters of the USDA Forest Service at Suite 800, 1720 Peachtree Road, Atlanta, Georgia 30309 and 633 West Wisconsin Avenue, Milwaukee, Wisconsin 53203, respectively.

APPALACHIAN TRAIL

Of all the trails in the East the longest and most popular is the Appalachian National Scenic Trail. More than 2,000 miles long, it travels through thirteen states from Maine to Georgia. In some areas it forms the backbone of other trail systems. It is well marked and described in guidebooks. Shelters have been built along much of its length at about eight-mile intervals.

This is a trail for everyone. Parts of it are difficult, while many sections are easy going. There are mountains to climb, streams to cross, meadows to stroll in, and cool forests to hike through. Some areas are real wilderness, other sections of the trail are routed through urban areas. Access points are numerous, making it feasible to hike the entire length, or take many day hikes.

Write the Appalachian Trail Conference, Inc., 1718 N Street, N.W., Washington, D.C. 20036.

TRAILS AROUND WASHINGTON, D.C.

While there are many short walks here to historic sites and monuments, there are also excellent trails for day hikes and overnighters.

These are primarily scenic in a pastoral sense; little of a wilderness quality exists along these routes. Write for *Potomac Trail Book,* Potomac Area Council, A.Y.H., 1501 16th Street,

N.W., Washington, D.C. 20036 for a comprehensive guide and maps to forty-five hikes in the area. $2.20 postpaid. From the same address ask for *C and O Canal Maps,* an edition of twenty-one maps describing the towpath from Cumberland, Maryland to Washington. $1.75 postpaid.

TRAILS IN MASSACHUSETTS AND RHODE ISLAND

Between them these states have over 1,000 miles of fine hiking trails. Most of these hikes are short, allowing hikers to spend a pleasant afternoon in and near small towns. Other longer routes take people into the Berkshires to more of a wilderness setting. Write for *A.M.C. Massachusetts-Rhode Island Guide,* Appalachian Mountain Club Mail Order, 5 Joy Street, Boston, Massachusetts 02108. $4.50 postpaid.

FLORIDA

Hiking in Florida can be an invigorating experience. Nowhere else do our nation's trails offer the uniqueness of primitive cypress swamps dressed with wild orchids, grassy savannahs swept by cool winds, broad prairies of palmetto, and rolling hills covered with pine forests. Wildlife is everywhere. Deer greet the dawn hiker, soaring hawks cry out in the blue above. And seldom is there no blue above. A bandshell sky stretches to all horizons. While the rest of our nation shivers in snow, hikers in Florida are removing their sweaters to soak up sunshine.

Foot trails are to be found all over Florida: in the midstate sandy hills and pines, in the central plains and range lands, and in the southern savannahs and swamps. The adventuresome and experienced can, with compass and maps, work out a route over abandoned roads, railbeds, creeks, and open fields, but most will want to keep to the marked trails found in all of Florida's national forests and state parks. Most of them are short, precluding anything more than an overnight trip. However, there is now a trail that extends the length of Florida, with long sections passing through these national and state forests. This is the Florida Trail.

THE FLORIDA TRAIL

Since its inception in 1965 the Florida Trail has become a 700-mile footpath extending from Tamiami Trail in southern Florida north to Panama City in the state's western panhandle. It is one of the longest trails in the country. At present writing about 300 miles of the trail have been cleared and blazed. The dedication and efforts of very singular men and women have made this possible.

Because much of the Florida Trail crosses private land, present arrangements with landowners make it necessary for hikers to be Florida Trail Association members. A nominal cost membership is available at Florida Trail Association, 33 S.W. 18th Terrace, Miami, Florida 33129. Other privileges come with this membership: periodic trail news, maps, information about conducted hikes, etc.

Where the Florida Trail passes through state or federal preserves, forests, etc., membership is not required. The trail section described below (Ocala Trail) is on public land.

OCALA TRAIL

The Ocala Trail is a 62-mile section of the Florida Trail. Hikers will walk the backbone of Florida, on some thirty feet of ancient, drifting sands that now cover a limestone bed. Below are a myriad of springs and underground rivers. This abundance of water helps maintain the healthy flora and fauna of the area. Tall pines and oaks ring the small prairies and over sixty lakes and ponds. The world's largest stand of the short-lived sand pine is found here. Junglelike fern, vines, and cabbage palms crowd the great oaks and pines in this land of semi-tropical growth. And in the forest deer, raccoons, opossums, foxes, and other animals make their home. Wading birds, ospreys, and eagles are seen by the lakeside. In fall and spring the woods are filled with the songs of migrating birds.

This is a pleasant hike, the trail level and easy going. It is well marked. Boardwalks have been constructed through swampy areas.

Water is plentiful; so there is no need to carry a full canteen, but water purification is absolutely essential when using water other than approved.

Permits are not required. Camp can be made anywhere, but good drinking water sometimes limits the campsite choices.

Season   This is shirt-sleeve hiking country. In winter you can plan on warm days and chilly nights. The season is generally October through May.

Location   The Ocala Trail is in the Ocala National Forest just east of Ocala, 40 miles west of Daytona Beach and 40 miles north of Orlando.

Access   Clearwater Lake Campground is the southern terminus of the trail, 16 miles west of Deland on State 42. The northern terminus is Rodman Dam. The trail crosses State 40 at Juniper Springs, State 314 and 316 west of Lake Ker.

Transportation Services   Bus service on State 40.

Accommodations   Motels in Ocala, Silver Springs, and Deland. Private and public campgrounds surround the area.

Medical Assistance   Deland and Ocala.

Fishing   Bass and panfish in all the lakes and rivers. Buy a license locally or write Florida Game and Fresh Water Commission, Tallahassee, Florida 32304.

Hunting Deer, bear, wild pig, and turkey. For seasons, licenses, and limits write above address.

Recreation On the trail those interested in wildlife, especially birds, will find ample specimens. Migrating and wintering birds, along with Florida's own varieties, are numerous enough to keep busy the most enthusiastic bird-watcher and photographer. Early morning is best for deer, late evening for raccoon, fox, wild pig, and other night prowlers.

For those hikers who might want to combine their outing with a more fashionable vacation there is Disney World in nearby Orlando. Silver Springs, with its glass bottom boats and deer farm, is near Ocala. The broad beaches of Daytona Beach are just west of the forest.

Reference For information about the Ocala Trail section of the Florida Trail write or visit District Ranger, Lake George Ranger District, Ocala, Florida 32670. Ask for the Forest Service map of the Ocala National Forest.

Trip Outlines

Trip A 30 miles, one-way hike: 2½ days, 2 nights
Start at Clearwater Lake Campground. Pick up orange blazes on right of entrance road to campground. Trail leaves this road shortly to the right, passes a sign directing hikers to Juniper Springs, and heads into the woods. Cross dirt road near fire tower. After about 2 miles cross F.S. Road 38. Continue on to cross another dirt road east from F.S. Road 38. Skirt lake and hike under power lines. Reach F.S. Road 39 and swing northwest to hike parallel with F.S. Road 38. Alexander Springs Creek is on right through woods. After 11 miles reach cutoff to Alexander Springs. Take this blue-blazed trail about a half-

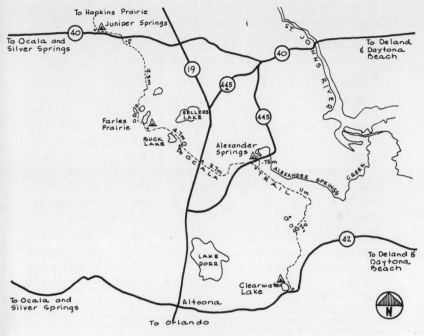

Trail Map for Trip A

mile to cross State 445 and enter Alexander Springs Recreational Area. Camp here. 11½ miles.

Second Day. Retrace steps to State 445 and hike west on highway to where trail crosses just before reaching dirt F.S. Road 38 on left. Continue north to round the south end of Billies Bay and turn south for a stretch. Presently turn north-west and cross State 19. Cross dirt road and reach ponds and then Buck Lake. Pump water here. Leave Buck Lake area and hike to Farles Prairie with its many ponds and lakes. Wonderful campsites at the north end of the prairie. Camp here. 12 miles.

Third Day. Continue north from the prairie to cross State 40 and reach Juniper Springs Recreational Area. 6½ miles.

Observations   Cars can be parked at Juniper Springs and Clearwater Lake Campgrounds. Or base at Juniper Springs and secure a ride to Clearwater Lake to start hike.

Trip B   20 miles, return trip: 2 days, 1 night
Start at North Hunt Headquarters at State 316 and F.S. Road 88 intersection. Trail is west of the corner by about 200 yards. Enter woods headed south through longleaf pines. Open hiking and very pleasant. Cross dirt roads several times and reach State 314. Then reach paved F.S. Road 88. Cross dirt roads again and reach north end of Hopkins Prairie. Hike into prairie and choose any one of a number of beautiful campsites. 10 miles.

Trip C   12 miles, return trip: 1 day
Start as in Trip B but go north on the trail. Cross F.S. Road 88 and hike around Grassy Pond. Campsite here. Cross dirt road and enter into pleasant parklike woods of longleaf pines. Reach Lake Delancy and campground. Lunch here. 6 miles. Return to parked car in the afternoon.

Observations   This makes a good overnighter if no one is in a hurry. Late evening fishing might be good at the lakes.

EVERGLADES NATIONAL PARK

This fabled "river of grass" covers 1,400,000 acres. Embracing jungles, swamps, and savannahs, it is a subtropical wilderness teeming with wildlife. Hikers on its 44 miles of trails should be on the lookout for alligators. Sportsmen will enjoy the saltwater fishing the park affords.

Map-brochures may be obtained by writing to Everglades National Park, P.O. Box 279, Homestead, Florida 33030.

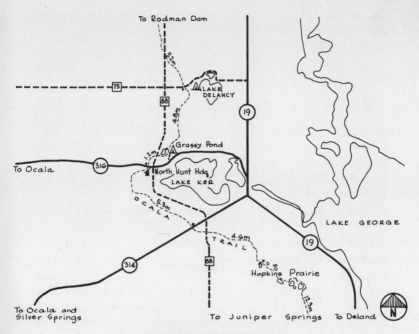

Trail Map for Trips B and C

NORTH CAROLINA

North Carolina is a favorite for many vacationers. The highest mountains in the East, cool summer temperatures, and a number of scenic attractions draw millions of people every year. The fine beaches of Cape Hatteras and the coastal marshes, the historied cities of Asheville and Raleigh, are only some of the places that can make a North Carolina vacation enjoyable.

However, none of these places appeal to people as much as do the western Blue Ridge and Smoky Mountains. Summer and winter sports are popular pastimes here. Of interest to the hiker are the hundreds of miles of trails in the mountainous region. Some of the best trails are found in Great Smoky Mountains National Park.

GREAT SMOKY MOUNTAINS NATIONAL PARK

A virtually unspoiled 800 square miles of mountain wilderness awaits the outdoorsman here. This is a land of rounded peaks topping 6,000 feet, dense forests, and rushing streams draining to lakes, ponds, and rivers. Heavy rainfalls green the mountains and misty valleys. Woodland trails are routed through rhododendron and mountain laurel, through virgin forests of giant trees and the magnificence of spring and autumn colors.

Season   Spring, summer, and fall.

Location   Great Smoky Mountains National Park is located in western North Carolina on its border with Tennessee.

Access   U.S. 441 passes through the park. Interstate 40 and 26 bring traffic to the area from the east and south. Interstate 75 services the north border.

Transportation Services   Bus service to Cherokee and Gatlinburg.

Accommodations   Hotels, motels, and resorts surround the park. Cherokee and Gatlinburg have complete facilities for visitors. Private and public campgrounds are found in and around the park.

Medical Assistance   Park first aid. Private assistance in Cherokee or Gatlinburg.

Fishing   Trout in some of the 600 miles of streams. Native brook at higher elevations. State license required. Buy one locally or write Wildlife Resources Commission, P.O. Box 2919, Raleigh, North Carolina 27602.

Hunting None.

Recreation Few people visit the park without making stops at the towns of Gatlinburg or Cherokee. Both offer the usual tourist attractions with the flavor of a pioneer town and Indian history.

Within the park are several points of interest. A ride to Clingman's Dome and then a hike up to the observation tower is something to include in any visit here. And so it is with a casual stroll, or drive into Cades Cove, where the past in these mountains has been restored. Nor should anyone miss the rebuilt farm display at the Oconaluftee Visitor's Center on the east side of the park.

Leading from this same entrance is the beginning of the Blue Ridge Parkway, a unique summit road. No signs, no power poles, no speeding traffic. Countless turnoffs to scenic views. This is the finest example in America of what can be done to improve the experience of pleasure driving.

Park Trails Over 650 miles of trails have been developed in the park. They offer a chance to see this wilderness on a week-long trip or a pleasant day hike. Many self-guided nature trails have been created. To provide a visitor with a better understanding of this region, there are short nature walks conducted by park naturalists.

The Appalachian Trail forms the backbone of the trail system in the park. It passes through the park east to west for about 70 miles. It can be hiked in a week. Trailside shelters are located at about a day's hike apart. Wood is scarce, so carry a stove.

Other trails in the park are in good condition and signed.

Water is plentiful.

Permits are required when not camping in designated areas.

References Write for map-brochure, *Great Smoky Mountains National Park,* Great Smoky Mountains Natural History Association, Gatlinburg, Tennessee 37738. Also ask for the topographical map of the park. $1.25 postpaid.

From the same address can be had an excellent guide to many of the trails in the park: *Hiking in the Great Smokies,* $1.25 postpaid.

Trip Outline

Trip A   20 miles, loop hike: 2 days, 1 night
Start hike at Smokemont Campground (2200). Take road beyond the campground and follow Bradley Fork upstream. This will be a 3,000-foot climb in about 8 miles. After about 5 miles, reach fork in trail. Bear right and start climb alongside Taywa Creek to Hughes Ridge. Reach Hughes Ridge Trail (5000). Turn left and hike to the shelter at Pecks Corner. Spring here. Camp here. 9 miles.

Second Day. Retrace steps along Hughes Ridge Trail. Pass trail down to Taywa Creek and Bradley Fork. Continue on out on ridge. Pass trail on left to Straight Fork and Big Cove. Pass trail on right to Smokemont and continue out to Becks Bald. Descend steeply to Smokemont Campground entrance and parked car. 11 miles.

Trip Outlines for Hiking Mt. LeConte   A very pleasant overnight hike can be had to the LeConte Lodge atop Mt. LeConte. This is an easy day trip to the lodge. Advance reservations should be made. For rates and information write LeConte Lodge, Gatlinburg, Tennessee 37738. There is also a shelter for twelve here. Five trails lead to LeConte. The trail data here pertains to two of the routes.

Trip B   14 miles, loop hike: 2 days, 1 night
Park car at Cherokee Orchard (2500) and take trail up LeConte Creek. Stiff hiking to Rainbow Falls. Fine lunch stop. Continue climbing. Reach trail on right leading out to

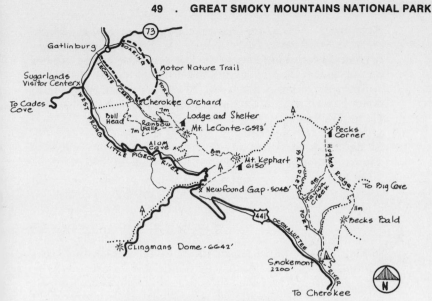

Trail Map for Trips A, B, and C

Bull Head and back down to parked car. Keep left and pass trail on right leading down to Alum Cave. Continue ahead and reach lodge and shelter. Spend the night here. 7 miles.

Second Day. Retrace steps to trail leading left to Bull Head. Descend to reach trail coming from Sugarlands. Keep right and return to parked car. 7 miles.

Trip C   16 miles, return trip: 2 days, 1 night
Park car at Newfound Gap (5048) and take Appalachian Trail east toward Mt. Kephart. Before reaching Mt. Kephart take Boulevard Trail left and the ridge to Mt. LeConte. This is a wonderful trail with many fine views of rugged Smoky Mountains scenery. Stay at lodge or shelter. 8 miles.

Second Day. Return to car at Newfound Gap.

WILDERNESS AND PRIMITIVE AREAS

Several other hiking areas are close to Great Smoky Mountains National Park. They provide paths to scenic beauty and remote places away from the more popular hiking trails. Among these areas are Shining Rock Wilderness and Linville Gorge Wilderness. Information about both these wilderness areas can be obtained by writing the southern regional headquarters of the USDA Forest Service at the following address: Suite 800, 1720 Peachtree Road, Atlanta, Georgia 30309.

SHINING ROCK WILDERNESS

Shining Rock Wilderness consists of 13,600 acres in the Pisgah National Forest. It is located just south of Asheville and bordering the Blue Ridge Parkway. The mountain, Shining Rock, is an outcropping of white quartz. All the land is above 3,000 feet. Cold Mountain rises to 6,030 feet.

Here are exceptional trout streams, many beautiful waterfalls, an unusual variety of trees, shrubs, and wildflowers, and an outstanding habitat for wildlife. Many miles of trails allow hikers to plan day hikes or long weekend outings.

The trails are blazed and signed. Water is plentiful. No permits are required.

Write for the map-brochure, *Shining Rock Wilderness,* Forest Supervisor, Pisgah National Forest, P.O. Box 2750, Asheville, North Carolina 28802. Also ask for the map-brochure of Pisgah National Forest.

LINVILLE GORGE WILDERNESS

Linville Gorge Wilderness, although only 7,600 acres, is really unique. The Linville River has carved out a steep-walled gorge for 12 miles as it descends over 2,000 feet from Grandfather Mountain to the Catawba Valley.

For the hiker there are many wonderful views of ridges, rocky spires, massive boulders, and overhanging cliffs. Trails pass through virgin forests of oak and pine, black locust, ash, and others. This is an excellent place for day hikes and overnighters.

Trails are blazed and signed. No permits are required. Water is plentiful.

Write for map-brochure, *Linville Gorge Wilderness,* same address as above.

JOYCE KILMER MEMORIAL FOREST

This very small wilderness of 3,800 acres is located in extreme western North Carolina within the Nantahala National Forest. This is an excellent place for day hikes and overnight trips. Two looping routes take hikers through virgin forests, rhododendron and mountain laurel, countless streams, over ridgetops and saddles, and a remoteness that is truly impressive for the East.

Write for the map-brochure, *Joyce Kilmer Memorial Forest,* Forest Supervisor, Nantahala Forest, P.O. Box 2750, Asheville, North Carolina 28802.

KENTUCKY

CUMBERLAND GAP NATIONAL HISTORICAL PARK

Among the prime attractions for hikers in Kentucky is Cumberland Gap National Historical Park. Deer, bobcat, and fox inhabit the mountains and forests of the 20,000-acre park, which contains 42 miles of trails. There is no fishing in the park, and water must be purified.

For map-brochures write Cumberland Gap National Historical Park, P.O. Box 840, Middlesboro, Kentucky 40965.

TRAILS NEAR CITIES

To find which trails are within about three hours' driving distance from major Kentucky cities, consult Finding Foot Trails Near a City in the front of this book.

VIRGINIA

SHENANDOAH NATIONAL PARK

The state of Virginia possesses fine hiking trails in the Shenandoah National Park, 300 square miles in the heart of the Blue Ridge Mountains of Virginia. These forested mountains rising above misty valleys offer countless recreational opportunities for visitors. It is a land of spectacular waterfalls, steep mountain slopes, and clear streams rushing through hardwood forests.

One-third of our nation's population can reach these wonders in a few hours. Motoring the length of Shenandoah along the Skyline Drive or hiking the Appalachian Trail, one will seldom drop below 3,000 feet. The park is open all year, although some of the facilities have a season; generally May through October.

For the most part, the exposed mountain rocks are ancient gneisses and granites dating back a billion years. In the Shenandoah Valley are the sedimentary sandstones, shale, and limestone. Shale and sandstone still cap a few mountains in the northern and southern sections of the park.

Common to the park are the gray fox, skunk, and raccoon. Black bear are scarce but deer are not. With an average of four to the square mile, the chances of seeing deer are excellent, especially for the hiker.

In the spring and early summer the mountains are colored profusely with blooming rhododendron, mountain laurel, azalea, snow trillium, and hepatica. This continues into the summer, with the trails and roadside bordered with Turk's cap lily, blueweed, and thimbleberry. The display of fall colors is inspiring when seen from trails or the Skyline Drive overlooks.

Season   Spring, summer, and fall.

Location   Shenandoah National Park is located in western Virginia in the Blue Ridge Mountains. The Skyline Drive traverses it north-south. Crossing it are U.S. 33 and 211. Interstate 66 and 81 service the north end of the park, while Interstate 64 services the south end.

Access   Most trail heads in Shenandoah are at some point along the Skyline Drive. Overlooks, campgrounds, or gated turnoffs at Forest Service roads provide parking areas for cars.

Transportation Services   None

Accommodations   Campgrounds and lodges in the park. Hotels and motels on any of the major highways bordering and crossing the park.

Medical Assistance   Park Ranger first aid. Private assistance in Waynesboro, Harrisonburg, Luray.

Fishing   Trout on artificial lures only. Good fishing in Jeremy's Run, Rapidan River, Piney Branch, Thorton River, and Big Run. Check with park concessionaires about a 3-day, $3.00 license.

Hunting   None

Recreation   Aside from the numerous scenic attractions in the park (Stoney Mountain, The Swamp, Mary's Rock,

Hawks Bill Mountain, White Oak Canyon, and others), with their trails and hikes, there are in the vicinity commercial enterprises like the caverns of Massanutten, Luray, and Skyline. Our nation's capital is within two hours' drive, and historic Civil War battlefields surround the park.

References Shenandoah National Park, set of 3 colored topographical maps (northern, central, and southern sections), $2.00. Potomac Appalachian Trail Club, 1718 N Street, N.W., Washington, D.C. 20036.

7½-minute quadrangles: Big Meadows, Fletcher, and Elkton East.

Circuit Hikes in Shenandoah National Park. 50¢. Address as above.

There are publications of interest displayed in the Visitor's Center at Dickey Ridge and Big Meadows.

Shenandoah Trails For the most part the trails in Shenandoah are blazed, easily found, and in good hiking condition. The trails are mostly restricted to foot travel, although fire roads are an important part of the network. Junctions are well marked and mileage to next junction indicated.

The water is unpolluted and safe to drink.

Shelters exist along the Appalachian Trail, but trail camping is limited to designated areas. A camping-fire permit is required, obtained at any Visitor's Center or campground. Backcountry fires are not allowed in the fire season, October 15 to December 15 and March 1 to May 15. Use stoves.

Hiking can be anything from leisurely to very strenuous. The elevation changes sometimes are great, and most of this is accomplished without the aid of trail switchbacks. In a park of this kind there are many good trips to be made by the backpacker, novice or pro. Following are three hikes chosen from the central section of the Shenandoah National Park.

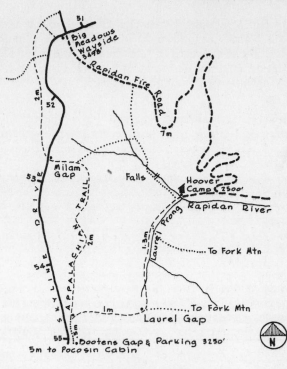

Trail Map for Trip A

Trip Outlines

Trip A 14½ miles, loop hike: 2 days, 1 night
Base at Big Meadows Campground at Skyline Drive milepost
51 or park car at nearby Big Meadows Wayside. Across the
Skyline Drive take the Rapidan Fire Road leading through
the open fields of Big Meadows. Ahead is a view of Fork
Mountain and its radio tower. At 1 mile pass chain gate. Good
views of Fork Mountain, Doubletop Mountain, and the
Rapidan River Valley are to be had from this road as it winds

downstream through the forest another 5 miles to join a dirt
road leading uphill. Take this route up. The Rapidan River is
on the left. Reach the Hoover Camp 7 miles after starting. The
Hoover Camp was the former president's retreat. Many of
the buildings have been removed, but the main lodge exists. It
is used occasionally as a VIP retreat.

Continue on to the west end of the Camp, passing the Park
Service sign describing the Hoover Camp. Take Laurel Prong
Trail about ½ mile to a designated backcountry camp area
amongst a grove of old hemlocks. Water can be had from the
Laurel Prong. Camp here. 7½ miles.

Second Day. Continue upon the Laurel Prong Trail. Pass
junction of Fork Mountain Trail on left (no longer main-
tained). Cross the Laurel Prong (fill canteen here), and start
steep climb to Laurel Gap. Another mile uphill brings you to
Hazel Top and on to the Appalachian Trail. Turn right to
follow Appalachian Trail north to Milam Gap. Cross Skyline
Drive and continue on for another 2 miles, crossing
Tanner's Ridge Fire Road. At the junction of the trail to
Lewis Spring Shelter, turn right for a ¼-mile hike to Big
Meadows Wayside and parked car. 7 miles.

Observations This trail is a moderate one. Only strenuous
section is the short rise to Laurel Gap. There is water about
halfway down the Rapidan Fire Road, a good lunch stop near
where Stoney Mountain Fire Trail comes in. Summer backpackers can usually get by with a wool blanket or a very light
sleeping bag at night.

Trip B   11 miles, loop hike: 2 days, 1 night
Park car at South River Falls Picnic Grounds between
Skyline Drive mileposts 62 and 63. Take Falls Trail down to
Appalachian Trail. Turn left on trail, cross South River Fire
Road, and continue on to rise north along Appalachian Trail
to Dean Mountain. Then descend to Pocosin Fire Road, 3½

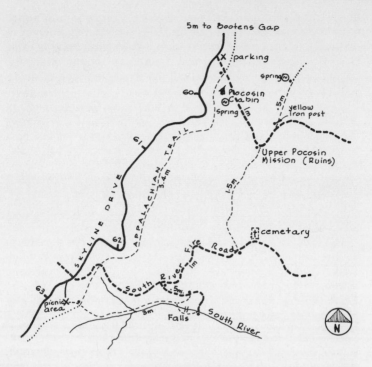

Trail Map for Trip B

miles from start. Turn right on fire road, pass Pocosin Cabin, and descend to junction of Pocosin Trail. Continue on fire road, turning left here, about ¼ mile until junction of Pocosin Hollow Fire Trail (yellow post in ground). Descend fire trail another ¼ mile to backcountry camping area. There is water here. 5 miles.

Second Day. Retrace steps to Pocosin Fire Road (yellow post) and uphill to junction of Pocosin Trail passed the first day. Now take Pocosin Trail (blue blaze) to South River Fire

Road coming in from the left. There will be a hilltop cemetery to the left. Bearing right, descend the fire road 1 mile to
where another road takes a sharp left downhill. Descend this
road ½ mile to a trail that goes to the head of the falls of the
South River. Cross over the river and descend steeply to the
base of the falls. Make this a lunch stop. Continue the hike by
retracing the trail to the head of the falls and continue up
steeply along the Falls Trail to cross the Appalachian Trail and
reach the picnic grounds and parked car. 6 miles.

Observations   This can be a very pleasant hike. The mileage
is short; the trail on the first day is mostly descending. It is a
hike that can be started late in the morning. The Falls Trail
will be a strenuous climb on the second day, but there will be
plenty of time to make it if the falls are used as a lunch stop
the second day.

Trip C   32 miles, one way: 3 days, 2 nights
Using the maps for Trip A and B, the following long hike can
be planned. Park cars at the Conway River Fire Road in
Bootens Gap, just south of Milepost 55 on Skyline Drive.
Park another car at the Pocosin Cabin parking area just north
of Milepost 60. Hike the Appalachian Trail north from
Bootens Gap to Milam Gap and Big Meadows. As in Trip A,
descend to Hoover Camp and start up Laurel Prong to camp
just above Hoover Camp as in Trip A. 12 miles.

Second Day. Ascend to Laurel Gap and reach Appalachian
Trail at Bootens Gap. Hike south along trail about 5 miles to
Pocosin Cabin Parking Area and descend via Pocosin Fire
Road and Pocosin Hollow Fire Trail to camp as in Trip B.
10½ miles.

Third Day. Retrace steps to Pocosin Fire Road and Pocosin
Trail. As in Trip B, take Pocosin Trail to South River Fire
Road and South River Falls. Then ascend to Appalachian
Trail at South River Picnic Grounds. Turn north on

Appalachian Trail and hike to car parked at Pocosin Cabin Parking Area. 9½ miles.

Observations This is a vigorous hike. Early morning starts are necessary. The first day, though 12 miles, is mostly descending.

WEST VIRGINIA

The Monongahela National Forest provides the backpacker with many miles of hiking trails. This 820,000-acre forest is located on the eastern border of West Virginia, along the Allegheny Mountains. It is a land of sprawling peaks and valleys, green forests, and swift streams. The forest is in the heart of the Middle Atlantic states, within 250 miles of one-third of our nation's population. A number of good highways pass through it east-west and north-south. For the backpacker there are several areas of interest. Principal among these are the Cranberry Backcountry and Otter Creek Backcountry.

These areas are open year round. Trail elevations make for cool hiking conditions during summer months. More rain here than anywhere else in the state insures healthy flora. The roadsides are lined with wild strawberries, the trails bordered with blackberry bushes. Dense stands of spruce and hemlock dominate the higher forest, and a heavy undergrowth of briars, ferns, and wild flowers covers the forest floor. The backpacker will probably encounter deer. Lucky hikers might see other animals: the very shy black bear, fox, muskrat, and beavers. To be flushed on the trail are grouse, quail, and perhaps turkey.

CRANBERRY BACKCOUNTRY

This 53,000 acres of forested mountains and rushing streams is restricted to foot, horse, and bicycle travel. Within it is a trail network that will allow a backpacker to stay on the trail for up to a week. These trails are made, in part, of old railbeds, abandoned and new logging roads, and fire control access roads. Because this is not yet a wilderness area, logging operations continue under permit. However, despite this, a high degree of isolation can be had by the backpacker.

Trails are designated with Forest Service Trail numbers and are blazed with blue paint: a small square above a vertical rectangle. Some are blazed with axe blazes.

Trails are easily hiked here; much of the mileage is over gently graded roads and railbeds. Nor are there any great changes in elevations. However, leaving the trail for cross-country is not recommended. Frequent encounters with brambles and brush make the going very difficult in open areas. Nor is following streams always possible; mountain laurel and rhododendron thickets make this almost impossible. On the ridges dense stands of spruce and hemlock are a barrier to progress.

Water is unpolluted and plentiful except on ridgetop trails.

There are several shelters in the area, most of them along the Cranberry River to accommodate the great number of fishermen attracted to the area.

Campfire permits are not required.

Season   Spring, summer, and fall.

Location   The Cranberry Backcountry is located in eastern West Virginia, north of Richwood on State 39.

Access   There are several places to enter the Cranberry Backcountry. The best of these is at Cranberry Campground, reached by taking the 12-mile F.S. Road 76 off State 39 just east of Richwood.

Transportation Services   Bus service on State 39.

Accommodations   Hotels and motels in Richwood. Monongahela National Forest Campground at Big Rock and Cranberry, both on F.S. Road 76.

Medical Assistance   Richwood.

Fishing   Best in late spring and fall. The Cranberry River is regularly stocked with trout. For license information write West Virginia Department of Natural Resources, State Capitol, Charleston, West Virginia 25305, or pick up license in Richwood.

Hunting   Deer, black bear, turkey, squirrel, grouse, quail. Check with above address for seasons, game, licenses, etc.

Recreation   On the trail the backpacker might be interested in searching for relics of other days when mining and logging flourished here. Off-the-trail finds can be remnants of stills, railbeds, and logging camps.

Near the Cranberry Backcountry are other attractions developed by the Forest Service. East of Richwood on State 39 is Cranberry Glades Botanical Area with its visitor's center and interpretive programs. This unique area supports life common to northern tundra zones. Close by on the same highway are the Falls of Hills Creek. A very scenic gorge trail leads down to three waterfalls.

Outside the forest there are touring attractions such as the coal mining exhibition and the outdoor musical drama at Beckley, with its dramas of old West Virginia. About 80 miles south of Richwood.

An exciting excursion can be had on the Greenbrier Railroad out of Ronceverte just south of Lewisburg. This day-long, 100-mile rail trip along the Cass Scenic Railroad travels through some of the wildest country in eastern America.

References   Map-brochure of Monongahela National Forest. District Ranger, Gauley Ranger District, Richwood, West Virginia 26261.

7½-minute quadrangles: Webster Springs SW and Webster Springs SE.

15-minute quadrangles: Lobelia.

An excellent study and trail guide is available. *Cranberry Backcountry,* West Virginia Highlands Conservancy, 407 Circle Drive, Hurricane, West Virginia 25526. 80 cents.

Trip Outlines

Trip A   19 miles, loop hike: 2 days, 1 night

Base at Cranberry Campground. With an early morning start from the campground secure a ride to Red Oak Knob Fire Tower, taking the cutoff just before the tower. Drive to gate. Take the North-South Trail (# 688). This is a ridge trail through mixed hardwood and hemlocks. Some spruce and birch. Carry water or rely on seeps along trail. Or drop off the trail to stream headwaters. Reach Birch Log Trail (# 207), an old logging road. Descend Birch Log Trail to Cranberry River Road. Camp here. 10 miles.

Second Day. Hike downstream along Cranberry River to Cranberry Campground and parked car. 9 miles.

Trip B   19 miles, loop hike: 2 days, 1 night

Base at Cranberry Campground. Take river road upstream to Birch Log Trail (# 207). Camp here. 9 miles.

Second Day. Ascend Birch Log Trail 2½ miles to North-South Trail (# 688). Turn left along the ridge trail 3½ miles to Lick Branch Trail (# 212). Descend 3 miles through hemlocks along creek to Cranberry River, and take the river road downstream 2 miles to Cranberry Campground and parked car. 10 miles.

OTTER CREEK BACKCOUNTRY

The Otter Creek Backcountry consists of nearly 30 square miles of forested mountains and streams. The area was com-

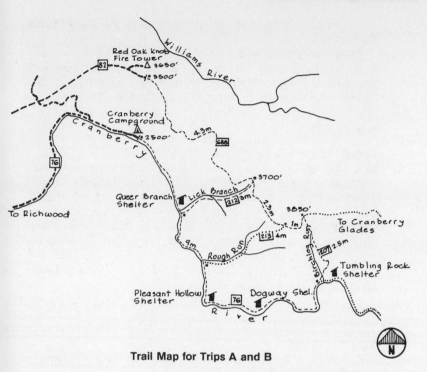

Trail Map for Trips A and B

pletely logged off from 1905 to 1915, then devastated by forest fires. It became part of the Monongahela National Forest in 1920 when the government started purchasing lands in the area to reforest and thereby protect vital watersheds and control flooding in the Ohio River system.

Unlike the Cranberry Backcountry, this area has no roads in it. One road presently penetrates a short distance. There are no logging operations here.

A network of trails allows a backpacker many days' travel without retracing his steps. All the trails are in good condition.

Old railbeds, abandoned logging roads, and pioneer foot trails make up this system of trails.

None of the trails are color-based, yet some still carry F.S. axe blazes. All the trails are well designated at intersections and starting points.

For the most part hiking is easy, the grades gentle. There are few switchbacks. Elevation changes are minimal.

The water is unpolluted and safe to drink. It is plentiful on the slopes, scarce on the ridges.

Only two shelters exist in this area, one on the banks of Otter Creek and the other on Shavers Mountain Trail. However, there are countless good campsites along the trails.

No permits are required.

Season   Spring, summer, and fall.

Location   Otter Creek is located in northern West Virginia, east of Elkins and just north of U.S. 33.

Access   Otter Creek can be entered on all its borders. On its southern border use F.S. Road 91 after leaving U.S. 33 at Alpena Gap Picnic Grounds. This is about 13 miles east of Elkins. As a base use Bear Heaven Campground, 4 miles from Alpena Gap on F.S. Road 91.

Transportation Services   Bus service to Elkins.

Accommodations   Hotels and motels in Elkins, Alpena, Parsons. Campgrounds surround the area.

Medical Assistance   Elkins and Parsons.

Fishing   The trout fishing here is not what it is in the Cranberry Backcountry. The natural acidity of the water is a drawback. To improve this condition in Otter Creek, there are limestone processing devices at its head. Pick up license in Elkins or Parsons. Or write West Virginia Department of Natural Resources, State Capitol, Charleston, West Virginia 25305.

Hunting   Deer, black bear, turkey, grouse, quail. For game, season, and licenses, write above address.

Recreation   On the trail the study of flora and fauna can be an absorbing one. Wet trails allow for good animal identification. This area is the finest black bear habitat in the state.

Scenic attractions in the area include the impressive Seneca Rocks, a sheer 1,000-foot-high quartzite formation thrusting up from the North Fork Valley, and Spruce Knob, the highest point in West Virginia at 4,862 feet. Private tourist attractions are Seneca Caverns and Smoke Hole Caverns. All of these are within an hour drive of Otter Creek.

Another must for visitors in the area is a trip to Dolly Sods Scenic Area, an unusual Arcticlike setting of 4,000-foot plateaus, upland bogs, and sparse forests. West of Petersburg.

References   Write for *Otter Creek Fact Sheet* and Monongahela National Forest map-brochure. District Ranger, Cheat Ranger District, Parsons, West Virginia 26287.

15-minute quadrangles: Parsons and Horton.

A very fine study and trail guide is available. *Otter Creek,* West Virginia Highlands Conservancy, 407 Circle Drive, Hurricane, West Virginia 25516. 50 cents.

Trip Outlines

Trip A   11 miles, loop hike: 1½ days, 1 night
Base at Bear Heaven Campground. Park car at end of spur off F.S. Road 91, 2½ miles from campground. This is the head of the Otter Creek Trail where it meets Condon Run (3200). Cross stream and take easy rise to Shavers Mountain cutoff (not marked), the first road to the right and down to Fishing Water Improvement Station. This is a limestone device used to reduce the acidity of Otter Creek and improve fishing. At the upper end of the sluice cross over to clearing and take abandoned road, now the trail. This can be found by skirting the edge of the clearing. The trail here is wet but a

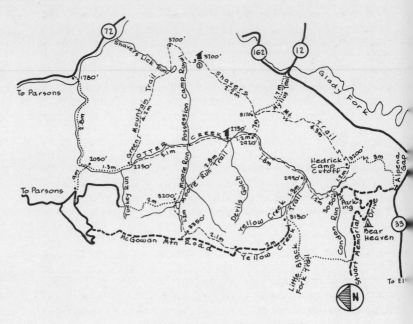

Trail Map for Trips A, B, and C

very easy rise. Many deer tracks along the trail. One mile from start join Shavers Mountain Trail coming in from right (3200). This is signed. Fill up a canteen here. Continue ahead and up moderately to steep switchbacks that lead to Shavers Mountain ridge. Road comes in on left. Stay on this and then leave to a rise through rocky outcroppings and ridge trail (3860). Here trail is marked with old Forest Service axe blazes. The trail follows the edge of a sheer dropoff to the valley below. Anywhere along here are fine views of the valley, winding Glady Fork, and Middle Mountain. Fine lunch stops. Cross over spruce forest knob with thickets of rhododendron and mountain laurel and descend sharply by switchbacks. Pass another fine valley overlook. At 5 miles reach intersection (3170) of Mylius Trail coming in from right, crossing Shavers Mountain Trail and going left and down 1 mile to Otter Creek and Otter Creek Trail. Descend easy slope to Otter Creek (2920), cross over to junction of Otter Creek Trail. Take a right downstream along the trail about 1 mile to make an early camp at the shelter (2750), just beyond junction of Moore Run Trail. Good swimming here. 7 miles.

Second Day. Return upstream along Otter Creek Trail. This will be a leisurely trip along an old railbed that seldom is more than a few feet from Otter Creek. Pass Yellow Creek Trail (2990) and reach parked car. 4 miles.

Trip B   20½ miles, loop hike: 2½ days, 2 nights
As above in Trip A as far as Mylius Trail junction (3170). Continue on Shavers Mountain Trail, climbing steeply to once again crest Shavers Mountain. Pass through a small stand of virgin hemlock in an understory of ferns and rhododendrons. This is fine ridge hiking. Reach the shelter (3700). Camp here. 8 miles.

Wonderful east views from here; Middle Mountain with Rich Mountain beyond. Spruce Knob (4862) to the south. A good spring north on the trail about 100 paces to a blazed tree on left, then west about 1,000 feet. Water from cistern at shelter must be treated or boiled.

Second Day. Continue on easy trail through spruce, hemlock, and hardwoods to junction of Green Mountain Trail (3700). Take Green Mountain Trail and reach high-altitude bog, headwaters of Shavers Lick Run. Continue on to descend very steeply (1,200 feet) to Otter Creek (2250). Take Otter Creek Trail upstream. Waterfalls, rapids, cool forest hiking here along creek. Pass Moore Run and Possession Camp Run. Reach shelter (2750). Camp here. 8½ miles.

Third Day. Continue up Otter Creek to pass Mylius Trail (2920) from left. Pass Yellow Creek Trail (2990) on right. Reach Condon Run and parked car. 4 miles.

Trip C   15 miles, loop hike: 2 days, 1 night
Start as in Trip A. Descend Otter Creek Trail to Yellow Creek Trail junction (2990). Take Yellow Creek Trail up to cross stream and hike through bogs. Grand view of surrounding mountains. Good lunch stop. Fill up canteen here. Reach divide (3150) and junction with Little Black Fork Trail on left. Reach end of McGowan Mountain Road. Hike road ascending or take Yellow Creek Trail where it leaves on the left about a half-mile from divide. Both meet again where McGowan Mountain Trail crosses the road. Take this trail north, ascending steeply to rocky crest (3870) and through dense spruce forest. Fine views of western ridges and Shavers Fork in the valley. Descend quickly through great sandstone boulders to reach junction of Moore Run Trail (3350). Descend on Moore Run Trail to bogs and Turkey Run Trail (3200). Camp here. 8 miles.

This is another high-altitude bog. The ancestors of today's flora were deposited here 10,000 years ago by retreating glaciers.

Second Day. Continue down Moore Run Trail. Leave the creek and descend through open hardwood forest. Fine views of Otter Creek Valley. Reach Otter Creek (2750) and turn upstream to pass Mylius Trail Junction (2920). This is all very casual hiking on an old railbed. Reach Yellow Creek Trail and then Condon Run and parked car.

OTHER WEST VIRGINIA TRAILS

Private and public efforts have developed other trails in West Virginia. Most of them are short, providing excellent day hikes or overnighters. The majority are routed through very scenic areas in the mountains and forest of the state.

Of special interest will be the trails in Cooper's Rock State Park, Dolly Sods Scenic Area, North Fork Mountain, Cheat Canyon, and Wolf Gap.

For an excellent publication briefly describing these and other trails in the state, write for *Hiking Guide to Western Pennsylvania and Northern West Virginia,* Pittsburgh Council, A.Y.H., 6300 Fifth Avenue, Pittsburgh, Pennsylvania 15232. $1.00 postpaid.

PENNSYLVANIA

Public forests of Pennsylvania comprise nearly 2.5 million acres of forested land. The largest single area is the Allegheny National Forest in the northwestern part of the state. This is a land of rolling hills and valleys with small streams meandering through hardwood forests. It is rich in Indian and pioneer history. The Senecas and Delawares were pushed from here when the white man moved west to settle and strip the land of timber. The Allegheny River on the forest's western border was once a busy waterway for trappers and loggers.

As in most of our eastern forests deer, black bear, fox, raccoon, muskrat, beaver, and small game of many kinds are found in this area. Grouse, turkey, woodcock, and many other birds can be identified.

Timber harvesting of hardwoods is carried on here. Of principal interest is the black cherry, which is prized by the furniture industry.

Over 55 million people live within a day's drive of the Allegheny National Forest. It can be reached easily from Interstate 80, which passes near its southern border. Like most of our eastern forests, it is cut up and bordered by highways. Forest Service roads complete the job of sectioning the forest.

A hiker cannot trek more than a few miles without coming upon some kind of road.

There is no network of trails in the forest as yet. However, there are several short interpretive hikes within the forest (see Recreation below). Under construction now is a section of the North Country Trail. When completed, it will be about an 80-mile route through the forest, with a spur to Tionesta Scenic Area. There is also the Tan Bark Trail running west from the North Country Trail.

NORTH COUNTRY TRAIL

The completed sections are in good hiking condition and blazed white with the standard Forest Service square above a vertical rectangle. However, the blazing on most of the trails is inadequate and will cause some anxiety. They are so infrequent that the hiker must always be checking. These are not convenience blazes, but rather like reminders for those familiar with the route.

In most places where the trail crosses roads there are wooden signs designating it the North Country Trail. Another wooden post is close by with a small metal marker: a yellow silhouetted backpacker on a black background.

There are no official distances available from point to point. Those given are approximate. Hiking time is given for a man with a pack averaging one mile per hour. This includes time to rest, eat, birdwatch, or just enjoy the scenery. Of course, it can be done faster. The trail allows a strong hiker to easily maintain two miles per hour.

There are countless places to make camp, many of them in very beautiful meadows or by the streams. There are no shelters.

Permits are not required.

Water is plentiful in springs and streams. Reports of its quality vary. So take your purification tablets.

This is pleasant hiking country, with very comfortable grades. The trails are used more by wild animals than men. You will certainly see deer, grouse, foxes, and a number of songbirds and hawks.

Season Spring, summer, and fall.

Location This section of the North Country Trail is in the southern part of the forest, north of Marienville on State 66.

Access Base at Beaver Meadows Campground, 5 miles north of Marienville on F.S. Road 128.

Transportation Services None.

Accommodations Hotels and motels in Marienville. Forest campground at Beaver Meadows.

Medical Assistance Marienville.

Fishing Trout in the streams. Bass fishing in the Clarion and Allegheny rivers, along with walleyed pike and muskies. For licenses write Pennsylvania Game Commission, Harrisburg, Pennsylvania 17120, or buy one locally.

Hunting For game, seasons, and licenses, write as above.

Recreation Pennsylvania is a state rich in pioneer history. Any good-sized town has a supply of brochures, etc., outlining points of interest in the state.

Of more than passing interest within the Allegheny Forest are two areas: the Tionesta and Hearts Content scenic areas. The Tionesta Scenic Area is a 2,000-acre portion of what was once a 6-million-acre forest on the Allegheny Plateau of New York and Pennsylvania. Hemlocks 400 years old and beeches 300 years old can be seen in this natural museum. Two interpretive trails lead to black cherry, hemlocks, and beech trees that were large before the white man ever reached the area. This attraction is 8 miles north of Kane on U.S. 6.

Hearts Content Scenic Area is 120 acres of virgin timber in a preserve south of Warren on State 337 and F.S. Road 18. Ancient white pine, hemlock, beech, and other hardwoods remind us of the forest as it once was.

References   Write for Allegheny National Forest map, District Ranger, U.S. Forest Service, Marienville, Pennsylvania 16239.

7½-minute quadrangles: Russel City, James City, Lynch, Marienville East, Marienville West.

Trip Outlines

The first four trips below cover a 19-mile section of the North Country Trail north of Marienville in four parts, east to west. The concluding three trips are based on the directions given for the first four trips. Consult the accompanying trail map for help in planning all seven trips.

Pigsear to State 66   7 miles, 6 hours
Park car at Pigsear sign of F.S. Road 125, south from State 66 where State 48 joins 66 from north, a mile west of Russel City.

From Pigsear sign descend to cross bridge. Trail marker is on right. Follow white blazes up gentle rise. Old oil well rig on right below. Reach fork in road. Bear right and descend. Cross stream. Road ends. Continue into dense forest on foot trail. Cross dry run. Cross stream trickle. Spring Creek on your right. Descend to stream and follow downstream. Meet trail coming in from left. Continue ahead downhill. Reach meadow. Cross wooden bridge. Tanks on left. Oil rigs. Continue to west end of meadow on road. Road swings sharp left and up here, but continue ahead. Cross small stream. Spring Creek on your right. Hike abandoned railbed. Meet road from left. Trail junction (another pleasing trail goes ahead along streambank). Turn right at sign of silhouetted backpacker on tree. Descend to stream and cross. Cross footbridge

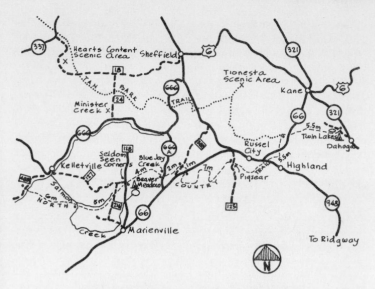

Map for Hikes on the North Country Trail

and ascend steeply. Level off. Descend and join old railbed. Spring Creek on left. Leave railbed and bear right to ascend into meadows. Cross meadows. Cross small stream and turn right. On old railbed again. Cross stream twice. Leave railbed and bear left to ascend. Trail comes in from left. Keep ahead. Cross wide seeping stream. Continue ahead. Leave stream and ascend into dense forest. Trail junction on rise (another trail goes ahead). Turn right here and continue to ascend. Reach clear parkway trail now grown over with grass. Still ascend easy slope. Reach level hiking along same road. Then easy descent. Reach wide gas line easement. Listen for pumping underfoot. Turn left and follow along easement. At bottom of hill where stream crosses easement, turn left down abandoned railbed. Reach great meadow and remains of virgin forest. Cross to south end of meadow (water here). Enter forest again. Cross streams. Reach meadow bending right with stream. Swing with stream (Rappe Run) to enter forest again, crossing at remains of old rail bridge. Stream on right. Continue along it and downstream. Cross stream several times. Reach clearing and continue to descend. Reach dirt road with bridge over Rappe Run. (Behind to left is abandoned oil rig. Dirt road crosses bridge and swings left and up.) Cross road and into forest. Rappe Run on right. Steel cables can be seen along left side of trail. Steel pipes on right. Cross stream; reach meadow. Cross wide stream. Reach pond and cinder railbed. Bear right and take cinder road to junction of road curving away left and right. Trail sign here. Bear on right fork of dirt road. Reach Marienville Rod and Gun Club's Trout Rearing Project. Continue ahead on railbed. Easy rise. Reach gas easement with pumping pipes underfoot. Turn right and follow easement about 100 yards. Listen for Spring Creek on left. Look for white blazes on left back in the forest. Pick up old railbed and trail here. Continue on railbed. This becomes F.S. Road 389. Pass houses. Highway noises ahead. Just before junction with highway look for trail turning sharp left to cross stream. Sign: State 66. Car parking is to the right across bridge.

State 66 to Blue Jay Creek   3 miles, 2½ hours
Trail access is about 9 miles north of Marienville on State 66 where bridge crosses Spring Creek. Park car north of bridge. Cross bridge to where trail starts on right. Trail forks immediately. Keep left. Join old railbed that will be the trail all the way to Blue Jay Creek. Stream on right. Climb through open woods. Balsam and spruce. Steady and easy ascent. Reach clearing. Reach sign: Waston Farm Road. Cross road. Cross railroad tracks and join old railbed. Railroad tracks on left. Pass turkey feeding station. Leave railroad tracks. Descending very easy. Reach small clearing. Another clearing.

Reach third clearing with standing dead trees girdled at another time. Huge boulders here, too. Old railbed follows along hillside. Cross seepage and small bridge. Reach clearing on right. Cross stream on wooden foot bridge into clearing on right. Reach sign: Blue Jay Creek. Cross creek and paved F.S. Road 19 to dirt F.S. Road 221 and parked car just south of Slater Run bridge.

Blue Jay Creek to Seldom Seen Corners   3 miles, 2 hours
Park on F.S. Road 221 just south of Slater Run bridge on paved F.S. Road 19 (detour State 666) about 9 miles north of Marienville.

Immediately leave F.S. Road 221 which goes ahead and up. Bear right, following white blazes on F.S. Road 10. Cross wooden bridge on Slater Run. Gentle rise through woods. Slater Run on left. Easy hiking here as through entire route. Pass mountain laurel. Reach fork in road. Junction F.S. Road 8. Snowmobile trail signs lead right. Keep left. Reach junction of dirt F.S. Road 9. Bear right on dirt road to where road ends and grown-over road continues on. Reach Slater Run Trail and pole gate. Snowmobile trail turns left. Keep straight ahead. There are no blazes in this section. Forest Service has widened the trail and cut down blazed trees. If you are lucky you will see the blazes on the downed trees. Trail gently swings to right. Reach fork. Sign: Beaver Meadows Recreation Area. Turn left here on F.S. Road 11 onto old railbed and into woods. Reach meadow with virgin forest stumps. Cross three wooden bridges. Reach F.S. Road 12. Turn left. Cross foot bridge into forest. Reach old railbed, now a road. Turn right. Cross steel pipe draining spring. Pass houses on left and right. Reach Seldom Seen Corners and F.S. Road 128.

One mile to left on F.S. Road 128 is entrance to Beaver Meadows Campground.

Seldom Seen Corners to Salmon Creek (F.S. Road 145) 6 miles, 5 hours

Park car at junction of F.S. Road 128 from Marienville and F.S. Road 127 turning west. This portion of trail well blazed. Credit Boy Scouts. Trail is to the left and behind private residence. Look for prominent white blaze on tree. Ascend moderately into forest. Reach fork; bear left. Reach fork; bear right. Trail comes in from behind on left. Reach F.S. Road 216. Cross into forest. At sign of silhouetted backpacker take sharp left. Reach sign: Greeley Farm 4 m. and Marienville 5 m. (this on F.S. Road 216). Bear right. From here on, the trail is probably the closest one can get here to a wilderness quality. Fork in road; bear left. Reach unmarked junction. Road goes ahead. Trail takes sharp left and descends, then ascends easily. There are faint yellow blazes here along with white. Descend gradually into meadow. Pass remains of old farm buildings and fences. Trail forks. Keep right and descend into woods on roadbed. Cross stream. 100 yards on, reach trail junction sign: silhouetted backpacker on post. Road goes ahead and down. Take sharp left and ascend. Boulders on right. Meet road coming up and from behind on right. Keep ahead on road now. 50 yards on, look for blazes on right. Trail leaves road abruptly; no signs. Descend steeply. Cross steel pipes. Reach creek; turn right around blazed tree and flat slab or rock. Cross creek and rocky trail to open overgrown field. Reach overgrown railbed. Bear left and up. Creek on right below but hidden. Continue ascending to junction of F.S. Road 165 and snowmobile signs. Main road continues left and up. Follow road downhill. Just before reaching bottom and stream, trail leaves road abruptly to left. No signs, only blazes. Cross stream at edge of forest. Sign: F.S. Road 145 and Salmon Creek 4 miles; F.S. Road 216 and Seldom Seen Corners 2 miles (not accurate). On this section cross many weeping springs and creeks. Creek below on right. Reach junction. Sign on tree: backpacker silhouette. Take right (other trail continues up to road). Trail very winding here but well blazed. Reach crumbling logs in stream. Fork in trail: take right. Descend to stream on right. Leave stream and ascend. Trail forks: bear right. Cross wide seeping stream. Cross another full stream. Reach meadow and virgin timber stumps. Trail is now in open woods. Leave meadow and ascend into woods. Level off halfway up ridge. Steep slopes to stream below. Reach end of ridge (trail turns sharply left and up). Take right here and descend by switch-backs in gap. Cross overgrown fields. Cross stream. Walk in open fields for about ½ mile. Enter open woods and ascend mountainside. Stream below. Descend to skirt meadow on right. Reach sign: F.S. Road 145. Salmon Creek bridge to the right on road.

Note: Six more miles of this trail continues west to F.S. Road 483.

The trail is also complete east from Pigsear to State 948 (4 m.) to State 66 (1 m.), and ½ mile to junction of trail coming west 5½ miles from Twin Lakes Campground Trail. Here the trail travels northerly about 11 miles into the Tionesta Scenic Area and ends at State 66.

Caution: pay particular attention to the blazes. Countless grown-over roads and trails peel off or run into this trail. It can be confusing. Rely on the white blazes even though you will have to search for them.

Pigsear to Salmon Creek   19 miles, one way: 2 days, 1 night
Camp either east or west of Blue Jay Creek.

Seldom Seen Corners to Salmon Creek and Return   14 miles, return hike: 2 days, 1 night
Base at Beaver Meadows Campground. Hike 2 miles out campground road and north on F.S. Road 128 to junction of trail at Seldom Seen Corners.

Pigsear to Seldom Seen Corners 14 miles, one way: 2 days, 1 night

Camp west of State 66. This could be a 32-mile, 4-day, 3-night return trip if base was Beaver Meadows Campground and trail was followed from Seldom Seen Corners to Pigsear and return (2 miles in and back, campground to Seldom Seen Corners). Camp first night west of State 66. Second night in Pigsear vicinity. Third night in first night vicinity.

TAN BARK TRAIL

A number of organized trails have been developed in Pennsylvania by private and public efforts. Some are on state lands, while others cross private holdings. These trails are historic and scenic, their routes often following the pioneering trails of explorations and commerce. One such trail is the Tan Bark Trail.

Close to where the North Country Trail enters the Tionesta Scenic Area the Tan Bark Trail starts to the west, traveling some 25 miles through the town of Henry Mills, touching the Circuit Trail at Minister Creek, bearing north to the eastern side of Hearts Content Scenic Area, passing Sandstone Springs and ending on the banks of the Allegheny River. It is blazed and signed at all road crossings. Check with District Ranger at Ridgeway for information about this trail.

SUSQUEHANNOCK HIKING TRAIL

This trail is an 85-mile loop through the Susquehannock State Forest in northern Pennsylvania. Once the hunting region of the Susquehannock Indians, an area rich in wildlife, it survived the arrival of pioneers only to have its virgin hemlock and pine wiped away at the turn of this century.

Now the forest has returned and is managed for timber harvest, water conservation, and recreation.

The Susquehannock Hiking Trail follows the route of the fire accesses, abandoned logging roads, and railbeds. Very little of the trail is on used roads. And few roads are crossed. It makes an oval loop with the east and west loops about 6 to 8 miles apart. Orange blazes, 2 inches by 6 inches, mark the route. Road crossings are signed.

There are no shelters.

No permit is required.

Water is plentiful. The trail is easy to hike. Elevation changes are minimal. 15-mile days are possible. Also cross-country hiking can shorten any hike to suit individual needs.

References Write for *Handbook of the Susquehannock Trail,* Potter County Recreation, Inc., Box 245, Clouderport, Pennsylvania 16915. Ask for the set of companion trail maps: $1.40 postpaid.

BLACK FOREST TRAIL

A few miles east of the Susquehannock Trail is another 40-mile loop route in the Tiadaghton State Forest. Both trails are now joined by the South Link Trail (6 m.).

The Black Forest Trail was named for the dense coniferous forests that covered the region before the arrival of loggers.

This is a high trail by Pennsylvania standards. The route has an average elevation of 2,000 feet, winding its way along mountainsides and over ridges, through oak forest and mountain laurel in the east; beech, maple, ash, and black cherry in the west. Good stands of white birch grow here also. Giant boulders, cascading streams, waterfalls, and broad vistas are all part of this very pleasant hiking trail.

The trail is in good condition and signed. Orange blazes mark the route.

Water is plentiful but should be treated or boiled.
No permits are required. Camp can be made anywhere.

Reference For an excellent map-guide booklet write for *A Guide to the Black Forest Trail,* Department of Environmental Resources, 423 East Central Avenue, South Williamsport, Pennsylvania 17701.

BAKER TRAIL

This trail is in western Pennsylvania, running 108 miles south to north from Freeport on the Allegheny River to Cook Forest State Park. Hikers will hike along streams and rivers, skirt ponds and farmlands, climb hills and stroll through meadows. This is comfortable hiking for the most part. Summer trips might be hot in open areas. A good deal of the trail is along dirt roads and highways. Private property must be crossed. Nevertheless, there are stretches of the trail that are strictly footpaths.

The trail is blazed yellow. Road crossings are signed.

There are eight shelters now with more planned. Most of the shelters have springs nearby. There are many sites to put up a tent.

Water is plentiful but most of it should be treated.

No permit is required. Respect private property. For an excellent guide with topo maps write for the *Baker Trail,* Pittsburgh Council, A.Y.H., 6300 Fifth Avenue, Pittsburgh, Pennsylvania 15232. 75 cents postpaid.

Reference Of interest to the Pennsylvania hiker will be a very good publication, *Hiking Guide to Western Pennsylvania and Northern West Virginia,* Pittsburgh Council, A.Y.H., 6300 Fifth Avenue, Pittsburgh, Pennsylvania 15232. $1.00 postpaid. This booklet describes briefly 100 trails in these two states.

LOYALSOCK TRAIL

A very scenic and rugged trail routes itself along 50 miles of ridges paralleling Loyalsock Creek in northeastern Pennsylvania. It starts at Montoursville on State 87 and goes east to Ringdale on U.S. 220. A number of side trails are either in existence or being planned in order to provide loop hikes.

The trail is signed and blazed.

No shelters, but there are excellent campsite locations with water.

Reference An excellent guidebook with maps is available from the Alpine Club of Williamsport, Williamsport, Pennsylvania 17701. $2.00 postpaid.

NEW YORK

New York State is a remarkable vacationland for the hiker. The State Conservation Department manages over 4.5 million acres of land. The largest of these is the 3.25-million-acre Adirondack Park, which includes a great part of northern New York. In the south is Catskill Park with more than 250,000 acres. The remainder is spread throughout the state in smaller management areas.

And in these lands there are over 2,300 miles of trails with more than 300 shelters for backpackers and canoeists. Access to some of these trails is made easier by the location of more than 40 public campsites.

Adirondack Park is made up of two natural areas: the Mountain Belt in the east and the Lake Region in the west. These rugged mountains are part of the oldest known strata in the earth's crust. Five parallel ranges contain some of the highest peaks in the East: Mt. Marcy (5344), Algonquin (5112), and Skylight (4920), all in the heart of this wilderness area.

The Lake Region in the west is a land of beautiful lakes and ponds connected by streams or short portages. These lakes drain south to the Hudson and north to the St. Lawrence. Trails in this area are numerous and for the most part easily hiked. This is also one of our nation's favorite canoeing spots.

Adirondack Park is located in northern New York. It is easily reached from any one of the eastern states. Interstate 87 leads north to pass the park's eastern border, and the New York Thruway passes under its southern border. Many fine highways lead into the park.

It is not difficult to find a wilderness trail in this area. The Mountain Belt and Lake Region offer excellent trails and scenic solitude. Besides frontier foot paths these routes are made up of abandoned roads and fire accesses. The mountain country will challenge the experienced hiker and offer the novice an excellent proving ground.

Many of the routes are dead-end trails to lakes or summits. However, loop hikes are found in areas such as those surrounding Mt. Marcy.

The trails are well designated with blue, red, and yellow disc markers. Trail junctions are signed, showing distances and ascents to other points.

The water is unpolluted and safe to drink.

Hikers are encouraged to camp at lean-tos, but it is not mandatory.

Fire permits are not required. Permits are required to make camp at one spot for more than three days.

Among the most interesting trail and hiking areas in Adirondack Park are Mt. Marcy, Cranberry Lake, Old Forge-Big Moose, Lake George, Schroon Lake, Blue Mountain Lake, and Northville-Lake Placid. They are described below.

MT. MARCY TRAILS

Mt. Marcy (5344) is the highest point in New York. It was known as *Tahawus* to the Indians. Not until 1837 was a recorded ascent made, and that a difficult climb through dense forests. Today Mt. Marcy can be climbed from all points of the compass, on trails designed to make the ascent a pleasant one.

Season   Spring, summer, and fall.

Location   Mt. Marcy is located in the northeastern part of the park, a few miles south of Lake Placid.

Access   The trails described here are reached from the north side of the park. Just east of Lake Placid, leave State 73 at a sign directing you south to the Adirondack Lodge, where camping and car parking is permitted for backpackers. This is the trail head for the ascent to Mt. Marcy and many other trips in this vicinity.

Transportation Services   Scheduled bus lines along State 73 to Lake Placid.

Accommodations   Hotels, motels, and campgrounds in Lake Placid. Camping and lodge at Adirondack Lodge at trail head.

Medical Assistance   Lake Placid

Fishing   Bass, pickerel, and pike in the lakes. Trout in the streams. State license is required. Buy one locally or write State of New York Conservation Department, Albany, New York 12201.

Hunting   For licenses, seasons, game write as above.

Recreation   Lake Placid is a resort town with all the amenities. Surrounding the whole area are countless villages at lakeside and in mountain valleys where vacationing hikers can include the "good life" in their visit to Adirondack Park.

Of historical interest is the John Brown Farm south of Lake Placid on State 73.

References   Write for *Trails to Marcy,* State of New York Conservation Department, Albany, New York 12201.

7½-minute quadrangles: Mount Marcy, Santanoni.

Trip Outlines

Trip A   17 miles, loop hike: 2 days, 1 night
From the car parking (2120) at Adirondack Lodge on Heart Lake take blue marker trail (Van Hoevenberg Trail). Reach yellow marker trail on right leading up Macintyre Brook to Algonquin Peak (5112). Continue ahead to turn right at caretaker's camp at Marcy Dam. Follow yellow markers. Pass leanto on right. Cross Marcy Brook. Pass leantos on right. Reach blue marker trail (2600) leading to Van Hoevenberg Trail or Lake Arnold Leanto. Continue on yellow markers ascending to Avalanche Pass (3000). Descend to Avalanche Lake (2683). Mt. Colden to the east and Avalanche Mountain to the west. Lunch stop here after 4½ miles.

Continue to cross lake outlet. Reach blue marker trail to Algonquin Mountain. Continue ahead on yellow markers. Reach Lake Colden (2764). Pass red marker trail to Mt. Colden (4714). At foot of Lake Colden reach red marker trail. Turn left and start ascent up Opalescent Brook on red markers. Reach yellow marker trail and take it left. Pass leanto. Reach blue marker trail to Lake Arnold and Mt. Colden. Turn right on yellow marker trail up Feldspar Brook. Reach Lake Tear of the Clouds (4200) and leanto. Mt. Marcy on left. Camp here. 9 miles.

Second Day. Continue on yellow markers ascending to Mt.

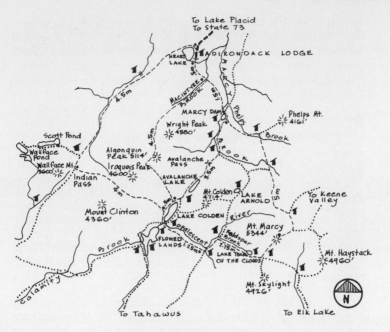

To Lake Placid
To State 73

HEART LAKE

ADIRONDACK LODGE

MACINTYRE BROOK

EAST

MARCY

Phelps

MARCY DAM

Wright Peak 4580'

Phelps Mt. 4161'

Brook

Scott Pond

Wallface Pond

Wallface Mt. 3600'

Algonquin Peak 5114'

Iroquois Peak 4600'

Avalanche Pass

Brook

Indian Pass

Avalanche Lake

Mt. Colden 4714'

Lake Arnold

To Keene Valley

Mount Clinton 4360'

Lake Colden

river

Mt. Marcy 5344'

Feldspar Brook

Opalescent

Flowed Lands

Brook

Lake Tear of the Clouds

Mt. Haystack 4960'

Calamity

To Tahawus

Mt. Skylight 4926'

To Elk Lake

N

Trail Map for Trips A and B

Marcy. Reach blue marker trail to Elk Lake and red marker trail to Mt. Skylight (4920). Bear left on yellow markers. Steep 1,000-foot climb here in ¾ mile. Summit of Mt. Marcy. Descend sharply from summit, on blue marker trail all the way to Adirondack Lodge and parked car. Red marker trail on right leads to Keene Valley. Pass 2 leantos. Yellow marker trail on right leads to Keene Valley. Yellow marker trail on left leads to Lake Arnold. Pass leantos. Cross Marcy Brook above Indian Falls. Red marker trail on right leads to Phelps Mountain (4161). Descend along Phelps Brook to Marcy Dam, following blue markers to parking lot and car. 8 miles.

Trip B   14 miles, loop hike: 2 days, 1 night
As in Trip A take road to Adirondack Lodge. Before reaching lodge, arrive at junction of Indian Pass Trail on right. Follow red markers. Pass leanto on shore of Heart Lake. This can be used night before trip. Small fee paid at Lodge. Reach Indian Pass Brook and leanto. Reach leanto and blue marker trail leading to Scott and Wallface ponds. Continue ahead. Reach yellow marker trail leading to Lake Colden Ranger Headquarters. Take this trail to rise between Iroquois Peak (4600) and Mt. Clinton (4360). Descend to Lake Colden. Reach blue marker trail. Camp here in one of many leantos. 8½ miles.

Second Day. Take blue marker trail north on west side of Lake Colden to junction with yellow marker trail leading to Algonquin Peak (5114). Take this trail and ascend steeply to summit. 2,300 feet in about 1½ miles. Descend from summit under Wright Peak (4580) to Macintyre Brook. Reach Van Hoevenberg Trail from Adirondack Lodge. Turn left and follow blue markers to lodge and parked car. 6 miles.

CRANBERRY LAKE

One of the finest wilderness areas in the state lies south of Cranberry Lake. Rolling hills, deep forests, lakes, ponds and streams without the scars of civilization characterize this region.

Cranberry Lake is located in the northwest part of the Adirondack Park. State 3 brings traffic to this area.

Fifty miles of trails well maintained and signed have been developed here. Cross-country hiking is possible by experienced backpackers and several good loop hikes are available from overnight to three days.

References   Write for *Trails in the Cranberry Lake Region,*

State of New York Conservation Department, Albany, New York 12201.

15-minute quadrangle: Cranberry Lake.

OLD FORGE-BIG MOOSE

This lake and stream country is in the western part of the Adirondack Park. State 28 brings traffic to the area north from Utica. The first road here was built in 1799, followed by steamboats on the lakes and then the railroad. It is now a popular recreation spot.

Some of the region's best is at the end of foot trails, away from the crowded lakeshores. The trails are short, but easy to hike. Day and overnight trips are possible. Few leantos; so take shelter.

Trails lead to good fishing and swimming, abandoned mica mines, firetowers on summits with scenic panoramas.

References   Write for *Trails in the Big Moose-Old Forge Region* to address under References above.

15-minute quadrangles: McKeever, Old Forge, Big Moose.

LAKE GEORGE

This is one of New York's most popular resort areas, located on the park's eastern border. It is well developed with motels, hotels, amusement and boating facilities. Interstate 87 and State 9N bring traffic to this lake.

The state has provided public campsites, parks, and picnic grounds. Most of the islands in Lake George are public, and thousands of acres of forest mountains surrounding the lake are state-owned. Into the more remote areas a hiker can backpack on more than 50 miles of trails, all well marked and signed. Excellent for day hikes and overnight stays. Leantos are conveniently located.

There are ridge trails, 2,000-foot summits, and trails following winding creeks, skirting ponds, and scrambling up to scenic overlooks.

References Write for *Trails in the Lake George Region* to address under References for Cranberry Lake above.

7½-minute quadrangles: Bolton Landing, Shelving Rock, Silver Bay, Putnam Mountain.

SCHROON LAKE

This is a grand region for hikers in the eastern part of Adirondack Park. Hilly lake country, good forests, and few roads make this one of the best in the state. No wonder it has become a major resort area.

Interstate 87 brings traffic north to the lake. U.S. 9 and State 73 also service the area.

Over thirty miles of trails are routed and well signed. Up to three days can be spent backpacking here without retracing your steps. Good fishing for trout, pike, bass, and perch.

References Write for *Trails in the Schroon Lake Region* to address under References for Cranberry Lake above.

15-minute quadrangle: Paradox Lake.

BLUE MOUNTAIN LAKE

Located centrally, and northeast of the Old Forge-Big Moose Lake region, this area is "high country" dominated by Blue Mountain (3769). Chain lakes, rushing streams, good fishing and boating make this a favorite vacation spot. It is easily reached via State 28 north from Utica or west from Interstate 87 and Lake George.

Forty-four miles of trails are maintained by the state. Leantos have been built at convenient locations. The backbone of the trail system here is the Northville-Lake Placid Trail (see below) that runs north-south around Blue Mountain. One-way or return hikes here. Loop hikes are out unless paved roads are used.

References Write for *Trails in the Blue Mountain Lake Region* to address under References for Cranberry Lake above.

15-minute quadrangles: Raquette Lake, Blue Mountain.

NORTHVILLE-LAKE PLACID TRAIL

This 135-mile forest route into the heart of the Adirondack Wilderness makes a good three-week trip. It can be done in two weeks by averaging ten miles a day, but that is pushing it hard. Or tailor the time on the trail to suit.

This is a blue-marked trail over footpaths, dirt roads, and highways.

Water is unpolluted in wilderness areas.

No fire permit is required.

Camping permit is needed when a stay is planned at one spot more than three days.

Carrying shelter will allow more freedom of campsite choice.

There are several points to get on the trail where it crosses highways or passes communities, making it possible to shorten time on the trail to a few days.

The trail moves northerly from Northville at the southern border of the Adirondack Park, through wild forests of the Adirondack foothills and rolling uplands, to reach the steep ridges and high peaks near its northern terminus in Lake Placid. It crosses countless streams and skirts picturesque lakes and ponds offering the fisherman excellent angling and a thoroughly enjoyable hike.

References Write for the booklet, *The Northville-Lake*

Placid Trail, New York State Department of Environmental Conservation, Albany, New York 12201.

7½ -minute quadrangles: Northville, Jackson Summit.

15-minute quadrangles: Harrisburg, Lake Pleasant, Piseco Lake, West Canada Lakes, Indian Lake, Blue Mountain, Long Lake, Saranac Lake, Santanoni, Lake Placid.

CATSKILL PARK

Catskill Park in southern New York was once an area of mystery to the Indians. Not until the twentieth century did white men begin to penetrate its wilderness to any extent. However, development was swift and relentless, with the result that now there is little of what can be called a wilderness quality about the Catskills.

Nevertheless, this is a beautiful land of softened summits and sheer cliffs rising from fertile valleys. Shale outcroppings are found on the lower slopes, while the summits are usually a conglomerate. Spruce and balsam cover the highest mountaintops; hardwood forests and some hemlocks dress the slopes and valleys.

The scenery is a wonderful collection of deep gorges, cascading streams, pleasant shaded valleys, and prominent peaks like Slide Mountain (4180).

Unlike the Adirondacks, this region has few lakes. The largest is the artificial Ashokan Reservoir on the eastern border of the park.

Catskill Park is located in southern New York. It is easily reached from any eastern state. Interstate 87 passes on its eastern border. State 17 passes on its southern border and State 23 on its northern border with State 28 cutting it in half. There is bus service to Phoenicia on State 28.

The Catskills are famous for their resorts and fun places. There is something here for everyone. And close by is lure of the big cities, their glamor and history. A hike in the Catskills by an out-of-state visitor can be combined with a few days sightseeing in New York, Boston, or Philadelphia.

Catskill Trails   There is little chance of hiking a Catskill trail without coming to an asphalt highway after just a few miles. Nevertheless, an acceptable degree of isolation can be had on some trails. Under these circumstances most hikers will be limited to two days. Longer trips can be made if the backpacker is willing to use some of the highways to connect the foot trails.

The trails are designated with blue, red, and yellow disc markers. Trail junctions are well marked, showing distances to next point.

It is best to consider the water condition in the routing of any hike. Certainly the mountaintop streams can be considered unpolluted. However, near communities and recreational areas it is best to carry water or plan on purifying it.

Hikers are encouraged to use a leanto, but camping is permitted anywhere. Some of these trails are heavily used; a tent may come in handy. Any stay longer than three days at one point requires a camping permit.

No fire permits are required.

Spring and fall will find these trails uncrowded.

References   Write for publication, *Catskill Trails,* State of New York Conservation Department, Albany, New York 12201.

7½-minute quadrangle: Peekamoose Mountain, Shandakin, West Shokan, Phoenicia for Trip A; Kaaterskill for Trip B.

Trip Outlines

Trip A   14½ miles, loop hike: 2 days, 1 night
Base at Woodland Valley Campsite. One mile west of Phoenicia on State 28, then 6 miles south on Woodland Valley road.

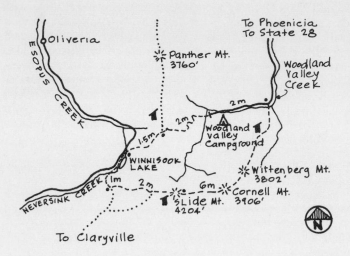

Trail Map for Trip A

Hike east 2 miles on asphalt road. Reach junction of Wittenberg Trail. Turn right and follow red markers across Woodland Creek on cable foot bridge. Reach registration booth. Pass leanto on right. Reach lookout to the east and north. Wonderful vistas. Ascend steeply, passing spring on right. Fill up canteens. Climb to summit of Wittenberg Mountain (3720). Good lunch stop. Descend to saddle between Wittenberg Mountain and Cornell Mountain. Reach spur trail on left leading to summit of Cornell Mountain (3880). Grand views of Slide Mountain. Descend to saddle between Cornell Mountain and Slide Mountain and start climb. Pass spring on right. Reach summit of Slide Mountain (4180) and leantos. This is highest point in Catskills. Camp here. 8 miles.

Second Day. Descend to pass Curtis Trail on left. Stay with red markers and reach junction with Phoenicia-East Branch Trail. Turn right and follow yellow markers. Leave old road and follow trail to highway. Take road to Winnisook Lake. Pass Winnisook Lodge. Leave highway at outlet of Winnisook Lake. Cross creek. Spring on right. Climb to divide. Reach junction of trail to Panther Mountain on left. Continue ahead and down to pass registration booth. Pass Woodland Club. Reach campsite and parked car. 6½ miles.

Observations   There is a lot of climbing on the first day, but well worth it. The views from the summits overlooking the Catskills are unsurpassed in the East.

A pleasant one-day hike can be made to Slide Mountain by parking at Winnisook Lake and taking a leisurely stroll south on the yellow markers of the Phoenicia-East Branch Trail. Then take the red markers to Slide Mountain and return. 6 miles.

Trip B   14 miles, loop hike: 1½ days, 1 night
This trip is along the Escarpment Trail, a winding cliffside route that provides spectacular views of Kaaterskill Clove and the Hudson River Valley. This is easy hiking; elevation changes are minimal. On a summer day it will be cool hiking at above 2,000 feet.

Park car east of Haines Falls on State 23A at Kaaterskill Creek Falls. Trail is on north side of highway.

Follow blue markers upstream through hardwoods and hemlocks. Branching to the left will be three different yellow marker trails leading to the falls and parking. Stay with blue markers and ascend to reach Layman Monument, the scene of a forest fire tragedy. Pass another yellow marker trail leading to North Lake road. Reach lookout over Kaaterskill Clove. Grand views of ravines and mountains to the south. Trail is along cliff edge. Reach Sunset Rock and view of Hudson River. Then Inspiration Point and a panorama of the

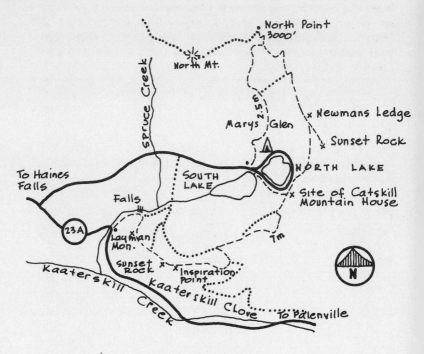

North Point 3000'

North Mt.

Spruce Creek

Marys Glen

x Newmans Ledge

x Sunset Rock

To Haines Falls

SOUTH LAKE

NORTH LAKE

Falls

x Site of Catskill Mountain House

23A

Layman Mon.

Sunset Rock x x Inspiration Point

7m

Kaaterskill Creek

Kaaterskill Clove

To Palenville

N

Trail Map for Trip B

Hudson River Valley from here on. Join old Kaaterskill Road. Then turn left and ascend on road. To the right is Palenville. Pass three red marker trails on left. Descend and reach historical marker of Catskill Mountain House Site. Pass along edge of North Lake Picnic Grounds. 4½ miles. Good lunch stop. Fill canteens.

Continue on ledge trail with blue markers. Steep climb. Reach yellow spur trail to Lookout Rock and Sunset Rock. This ¼-mile trail also makes a good lunch stop. Return to blue marker trail and reach Newman's Ledge. Climb to spruce trees and open area. Reach yellow marker trail to Mary's Glen and North Lake Campsite. Reach red marker trail leading to same places. Climb steeply to North Point (3000).

At this point retrace steps to red marker trail leading to North Lake Campsite. Pass through Mary's Glen and reach campsite. Camp here. 9 miles.

Second Day. Pick up blue marker trail at edge of picnic grounds and retrace steps to start and parked car. 5 miles.

Or leave blue markers where red marker trail bears right. Follow this trail to Kaaterskill Falls and descend along creek to road and parked car. 5 miles.

Observations This is a very busy trail. An early morning start will allow a strong hiker to get beyond the picnic grounds before the crowds get there, or plan trips for mid-week.

Bus line service on State 23A.

VERMONT

Running the length of Vermont is a trail that extends from Canada to Massachusetts, a 260-mile route through forests and over mountain summits. This is the Long Trail, a unique footpath that allows hikers to follow the ridge trail without carrying tents or tarp. Seventy shelters have been built at about 4-mile intervals. The Appalachian Trail joins the Long Trail from the east and New Hampshire.

The trail is blazed white. Junctions are signed.

Water is plentiful.

No permits are required.

The trail has numerous access points. However, there are few chances to plan loop hikes without using roads and highways. One exception to this is the Mt. Mansfield region in upper Vermont. Therefore most hikes will be return or one-way. Many delightful day hikes are to be taken on this trail.

The Green Mountain Club produces a complete and authoritative guidebook to the trail, a pocket-size edition with maps for $3.00 postpaid. Write for *Long Trail Guide Book,* Green Mountain Club, P.O. Box 94, Rutland, Vermont 05701. Also ask for the brochure, *Short Hikes on the Long Trail.*

For a map-brochure of Green Mountain National Forest, write Green Mountain National Forest, 151 West Street, Rutland, Vermont 05701.

NEW HAMPSHIRE

WHITE MOUNTAIN NATIONAL FOREST

Within this state is one of the finest wilderness areas remaining in the Northeast: White Mountain National Forest, a ¾ million-acre preserve that extends into western Maine. New England's highest peak, Mt. Washington (6288), is the focal point of this superb hiking country. Here there are hundreds of miles of fine foot trails and many shelters. The Appalachian Mountain Club, the oldest club of its kind in our nation, maintains 350 miles of trails. Also operated by them is a system of nine huts that provide overnight lodging and meals for hikers. No need to carry a tent or sleeping bag.

Season Spring, summer, and fall.

Location White Mountain National Forest is located in northern New Hampshire.

Access Interstates 91 and 93 bring people north to upper

New Hampshire and the White Mountains. From the west Interstate 89 and U.S. Highway 2 reach into the area.

Transportation Services   Scheduled bus service on State 16 and U.S. 302.

Accommodations   Hotels, motels, resorts on all the highways running through the forest. Public campgrounds throughout the area.

Medical Assistance   Conway, Gorham, Littleton.

Fishing   Trout in the streams. Bass, pike, and perch in the lakes. Buy a license locally or write New Hampshire Fish and Game Department, Concord, New Hampshire 03301.

Hunting   Deer, bear, grouse, ducks. For game, seasons, and licenses write above address.

Recreation   New Hampshire is a vacation state. Seashore and mountains are only a few hours apart. The state is rich in pioneer history, scenic places, and natural wonders. Some of the oldest homes in America are preserved here. Special attractions for vacationing children are Santa's Village on State 2 in Jefferson, or Story Land on State 16 in Glen. Mountain rides are popular. Ride the Cog Railway to Mt. Washington (6288) or the Cannon Mountain Aerial Tram in Franconia Notch. A cool summer walk can be had in Glacier Caves near Plymouth.

References   Write for map-brochure of White Mountains National Forest, District Ranger, Saco Ranger Station, Conway, New Hampshire 03818.
   15-minute quadrangles: Crawford Notch (S), Franconia for Trip A and Trip B; Mt. Washington, Gorham, North Conway, and Crawford Notch (S) for Trip C.
   Maps and guide: *A.M.C. White Mountain Guide,* Appalachian Mountain Club Mail Order, 5 Joy Street,

Boston, Massachusetts 02108. Send $6.25 for this most complete and authoritative guide to the mountain trails.

White Mountain Trails   The Appalachian Trail provides the backbone for many miles of loop hikes that can be made here. It comes into the forest at its northeastern border and leaves on the western border. However, many days can be spent in this wild, mountainous region without ever walking the Appalachian Trail. Moreover, numerous day hikes are possible. Trails vary from the easy to the very arduous, some for only the experienced.

There are countless places to pick up trails leading into these forested mountains.

Trails are in good condition and signed.

Permits are required for fire. Camps can be made anywhere.

Water is plentiful, except at ridgetops.

Following are suggested trips.

Trip Outlines

Trip A   30½ miles, loop hike: 3 days, 2 nights
This trail is routed into the Pemigewasset Wilderness and Lincoln Woods Scenic Area, a 19,560-acre tract of forest and peaks. Mt. Bond (4714) is the highest of these.

There are shelters in this area, but plan on tents or flies. It can be crowded, especially on weekends.

Kancamagus Highway brings traffic to the southern trail heads.

Take the Wilderness Trail where it leaves the Kancamagus Highway (1200) just east beyond the Hancock Picnic Area. The trail goes northerly following the bed of an old logging railroad. Very pleasant hike ascending the Pemigewasset River. Pass trail to Black Pond on left. Pass shelter on left. Cross Franconia Brook Trail on left. Reach shelter and then Bondcliff Trail, both on left. Cross river on suspension bridge.

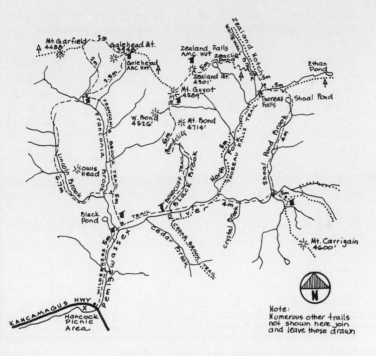

Trail Map for Trips A and B

Pass Cedar Brook Trail on right. This makes a good lunch stop after 5 miles hiking.

Continue ahead. Pass Thoreau Falls Trail on left. Cross Crystal Brook. Cross river twice (no bridge) and reach junction. Here Shoal Pond Trail crosses river and turns north. Carrigain Trail turns right to Desolation Shelter. Take this trail to shelter. Camp here. 9½ miles.

Second Day. Retrace steps to Shoal Pond Trail and take this north along brook to Shoal Pond. Reach fork in trail. Bear left to join Ethan Pond Trail (part of Appalachian Trail). At junction with Thoreau Falls Trail take sharp left and descend to Thoreau Falls. Good lunch stop after about 5 miles.

Retrace steps to Ethan Pond Trail. Turn left and hike into Zealand Notch and its fire-scarred walls. Reach Zeacliff Trail to left. Take this trail, cross Whitewall Brook, start steep climb to reach Twinway Trail, and turn left again. Hike up to Zealand Mountain (4301), passing Zeacliff Pond below on left. Descend on ridge between Zealand Mountain and Mt. Guyot. Ascend Mt. Guyot. Reach summit (4589). Descend to take sharp left on Bondcliff Trail. Descend on side trail leading to shelter. Camp here. 10 miles.

Third Day. Ascend from shelter to Bondcliff Trail and hike up to Mt. Bond (4714). Descend along Bondcliff open ridge. Leave ridge and descend sharply to reach Black Brook. Then reach Wilderness Trail and shelter along Pemigewasset River (1600). Lunch here.

Retrace route of first day, downstream to Kancamagus Highway. 11 miles.

Observation This is a very pleasant hike on comfortable grades for the first and third days. Second day has an afternoon of tougher hiking. Magnificent view from Zealand, Guyot, and Bond.

Trip B 18½ miles, loop hike: 2 days, 1 night
Start as in Trip A. Take Wilderness Trail up Pemigewasset River to turn left and follow Franconia Brook Trail. Hike old railbed. Pass trail on right to shelter. Pass Lincoln Brook Trail on left. Cross Hellgate, Redrock, and Twin brooks. Reach Lincoln Brook Trail coming in from left. Turn right on Franconia Brook Trail and reach shelter (2250). Camp here. 8 miles.

Second Day. Retrace steps and take Lincoln Brook trail to right. Climb steeply to a divide (3150); then descend along

Lincoln Brook and pass under cliffs on left to reach Franconia Brook and Franconia Brook Trail, thereby completing a circuit hike around Owl's Head Mountain (4023). Turn right and reach Wilderness Trail. Descend to Kancamagus Highway. 10½ miles.

Observation A very plesant hike. Fine for novices or a family with children. An extra day can be added by continuing on Franconia Brook Trail to Mt. Garfield (4488) and turning right on Appalachian Trail to Galehead A.M.C. Hut and a hot lunch. Take Frost Trail to Galehead Mountain (3948). Return and descend Twin Brook Trail to shelter. About 6 miles.

Trip C   19 miles, loop hike: 2 days, 1 night
The Presidential Range in the Great Gulf Wilderness is one of the most popular hiking areas in America. Here is stiff climbing to spectacular summits and panoramas. There are no trees, only rock and some scrub. Several miles of ridge trail, most of it above 5,000 feet, borders the Great Gulf to provide a unique hiking experience in the East. A memorable hike can be had by leaving some of that load at home and using the A.M.C. Hut System. Advance reservations (2 weeks) are required. No deposit needed. Send for the brochure *Huts of the A.M.C.*, North Country System Headquarters, Pinkham Notch Camp, Gorham, New Hampshire 03581.

Caution: This is high, wild country subject to sudden fierce storms, even in midsummer. Be sure to hike with adequate clothing, compass, and maps.

Park car at Pinkham Notch Camp. This is the A.M.C. Headquarters for the area. The Appalachian Trail passes through here.

Take the Tuckerman Ravine Trail from the camp. After about 100 yards turn right on Old Jackson Road and hike north, climbing to Mt. Washington auto road. Hike up road.

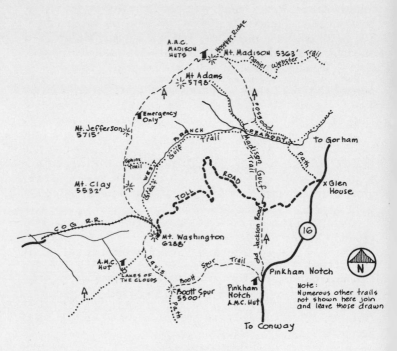

Trail Map for Trip C

Pass milepost 2 and reach trail leading to Lowes Bald Spot.
Now hiking Madison Gulf Trail. Pass trail to Bald Spot on
right (a short walk to wonderful views). Turn left here and
ascend to ledges and views of Mt. Adams. Then start descent
to pass Great Gulf Trail on left. Cross west branch of
Peabody River on suspension bridge. Turn left up the ridge.
Cross Parapet Brook and reach junction of cutoff from Osgood Trail. Leave Madison Gulf Trail and take cutoff to Osgood Trail (part of the Appalachian Trail) and spring. Fill up
canteens. Start ascent to Osgood Ridge and treeline. Trail

follows cairns. Pass Daniel Webster Trail from right at Osgood junction. Parapet Trail goes left along the south side of Mt. Madison. Continue ahead and up. Howker Ridge Trail on right. Watson Path on right. Reach Mt. Madison summit (5363). Descend to Madison Hut and lodgings. 7 miles.

Second Day. Start early and take Gulfside Trail (Appalachian Trail) west to Mt. Washington. Be sure to have adequate clothing; severe weather with freezing temperatures can occur at any time. Wind, fog, or sleet can bring a quick end to a trip and force hikers off the ridge. The trail elevation varies from 4,815 feet to 6,288 feet at Mt. Washington. This section of the trail is all open, affording matchless views of summits, great cliffs, ravines, waterfalls, and forested slopes. Many trails come into it and leave.

Mt. Washington makes a good lunch stop. Concession provides hot drinks and light lunches.

Continue west on Crawford Path. Pass Westside Trail on right. Reach Davis Path on left and descend it across Bigelow Lawn to Boot Spur (5500). Take Boot Spur Trail left and descend steeply to Pinkham Notch and parked car. 12 miles.

Observation   Without heavy packs this is truly a fine hike. Second-day mileage is mostly descending.

CHAPTER 3

TRAILS MIDWEST

FOR PURPOSES of this guide this region generally includes those states west of Appalachia and east of the Rocky Mountains. For the hiker trails in this area are scarce. A lack of public lands is the main reason few trails have been built. State and national forests are few and small in area. In most cases these lands are already crisscrossed with access roads. With the move west the plains were civilized and farms laid out systematically with their bordering roads. Nor does this land have what many people consider essential to a wilderness environment: mountains. The Ozarks in Arkansas are an exception to this but they, too, are mostly private property.

Louisiana, Kansas, and South Dakota offer little in the way of foot trails. Other states like North Dakota, Nebraska, and Indiana have little of the topography, flora, and fauna to attract the wilderness lover.

However, there are midwest areas where trails do provide

Mirror Lake in Porcupine Mountains State Park, Michigan

a wonderful chance to backpack. Michigan and Ohio have well-developed trail systems. Generally these routes are easy going in terrain with little change in elevation, although potable water is sometimes hard to find because of the proximity of civilization. Look for deep forests of hardwood, rushing trout streams, cool lakes, warm days, and balmy nights. The season is long: May through November in much of this region.

Illinois, Arkansas, Oklahoma, Wisconsin, Missouri, and Minnesota provide wilderness outings via water trails. The Boundary Waters Canoe Area in Minnesota is well known in this regard. For information about it, write Eastern Regional Headquarters, USDA Forest Service, 633 West Wisconsin Avenue, Milwaukee, Wisconsin 53203.

OHIO

Men have made of this state what many would like to see undone. The forests have been swept away, the rivers polluted, the cities and towns industrialized to the point where it is obvious too much happened to Ohio too quickly. Despite this there are places where a hiker can retreat to quiet and a scene that offers things of nature rather than man.

Topographically, the state offers the hiker rolling hills, lake country, valleys, and open farmlands. Rugged gorges and ridges are found in areas like the valley of Big Sandy Run and the Little Miami River. There is romance here in this pastoral setting, and Indian and pioneer history in the forests and along the canals that were once vital commercial routes.

Ohio has many hundreds of miles of trails, some privately organized and others maintained by state and federal agencies. The longest of these is the Buckeye Trail.

THE BUCKEYE TRAIL

This 500-mile trail starts in southwestern Ohio at Cincinnati, moves east under Chillicothe, and gently swings north to end at Lake Erie west of Cleveland. The trail is broken up into nine sections maintained by Buckeye Trail Association members in cooperation with private landowners, industries, and various government agencies.

The trail is marked with blue paint blazes, 2 inches by 6 inches, that appear on just about any object: trees, poles, posts, etc., close to the route. Two blazes, one above the other, note a change in direction. The blazes can be seen from both directions. Side trails are similarly marked with white blazes.

As much of the trail passes through private property, there are few organized or designated campsites along the trail other than where the trail crosses public forests and parks areas. None of the water can be considered safe. Boil water or use purification tablets.

The trail is mostly dry and very easy to hike; changes in elevation are minimal. However, the route has none of the criteria that would qualify it as a wilderness trail. Moreover, a hiker is hard pressed to find just a few miles of solitude. Almost the entire length of the trail can be driven by car on some kind of road. These roads are used regularly by vehicles. Long sections of the trail wind through suburban areas. Seldom is one away from highway noise.

For the most part this is open hiking, hot and uncomfortable. Perhaps early spring and certainly the fall would be pleasant for trips over rolling farmlands and the few forested areas. Winter hikes are popular here.

The trail can be joined at any point along its route. Any length trip can easily be planned. Good day hikes can be had in some of the rural areas, whereas the forested areas of the south would probably prove best for overnight trips.

Sections B and C are to be considered good sections to

hike. Much of the trail here passes through state parks and forests. Moreover, these two sections offer more campsites: 19 in a 136-mile stretch.

References The Buckeye Trail Association has developed maps for the nine sections of the trail. Using these, and the text that goes along with them, a hiker can follow this trail without much trouble. Maps are 25¢ each postpaid. Contact the Buckeye Trail Association, Inc., 913 Ohio Departments Building, 65 South Front Street, Columbus, Ohio 43215.

OTHER OHIO TRAILS

There are over 900 miles of trails sponsored and maintained by individuals and youth organizations in Ohio. Some of them make for excellent hiking. Much of the mileage is on off-road trails in sections that are more appealing to the hiker. Some of it is in rugged hill country or national and state forests. Many of the hikes are on loop trails. Contact the Ohio Division of Parks and Recreation, 913 Ohio Departments Building, Columbus, Ohio 43215 and ask for their information on the Ohio Youth Organizations Hiking Trails.

The state forests and parks have developed trails for hiking, horseback riding, and vehicles. In the parks they are mostly short nature, scenic, and interpretive walks. In the forests the trails frequently follow old roads. Nevertheless, they offer good day hikes.

Hocking Hills State Park has some of Ohio's finest trails along gorge rims, under great overhanging rock shelters, to waterfalls, cliffs and through rock tunnels. The Buckeye Trail passes through here.

Mohican State Park was once the hunting grounds of the Delaware Indians. John Smith was the first white man to visit the area, and Johnny Appleseed tended his apple trees here. Trails lead to falls, an old stage coach road, and a swinging bridge.

NORTH DAKOTA

Hikers in North Dakota should not miss Theodore Roosevelt National Memorial Park. Containing 70,000 acres, the park comprises badlands, mesas, buttes, ravines, and prairies. Wildlife along its 70 miles of trails includes bison, pronghorn, bighorn sheep, and deer.

For map-brochures write Theodore Roosevelt National Memorial Park, Medora, North Dakota 58645.

SOUTH DAKOTA

One of the outstanding attractions for hikers in South Dakota is Badlands National Monument. It consists of 244,000 acres of forbidding, rugged terrain carved into the Great Plains. This lunarlike landscape is great for fossil study. Wildlife within the Monument's boundaries include coyote, badger, golden eagle, deer, and pronghorn.

There are no trails; so all hiking is cross-country. Be sure to carry water. Summer storms can be extreme.

Map-brochures can be obtained by writing Badlands National Monument, P.O. Box 72, Interior, South Dakota 57750.

MICHIGAN

The state of Michigan has 6,400,000 acres of land in public forest ownership, more than any other state east of the Rocky Mountains. This land includes 29 state and 4 national forests. To a great extent these acres are managed to insure the complete enjoyment of the outdoorsmen of Michigan and America. The state is rich in pioneer history and Indian lore. Nations battled for this land once so rich in fur trade. At the turn of the century loggers stripped the land of its trees, and mining became an important industry.

The hiker will find most of the trails in Michigan forested with little change in elevation. There are numerous lakes to fish and streams to follow. While the Lower Peninsula does not offer wilderness conditions, it does provide fine hiking in the Michigan Riding-Hiking Trail. In the Upper Peninsula the backpacker will find good wilderness trails in the Porcupine Mountains.

There are many wild and remote regions in Michigan, especially in the Upper Peninsula. There are other places of singular scenic beauty, or quiet spots where a hiker can casually investigate and appreciate his natural surrounds. This chapter contains examples of each.

MICHIGAN HIKING-RIDING TRAIL

This 210 miles of trail winds its way across the northern part of Michigan's Lower Peninsula from Lake Superior to Lake Huron. It was developed by a co-ordinated effort from private citizens and government agencies. Most of the trail is on state or federal lands.

The western part of the trail traverses dune country and pine woods. In the east there are hardwood forests. There are many streams to cross and several lakes and swamps to skirt, with excellent fishing in some. For the most part this trail is on or alongside dirt and abandoned roads. In some places the route is through a pastoral and rural setting, while in others it is suburban. However, there are areas in the public forests that provide seclusion for the hiker. And in these places are the largest concentration of wildlife. Most likely to be seen on the trail are deer and raccoon. Some areas still support black bear and bobcats. A variety of birds fill the forests.

The trail is easily hiked with minimal changes in elevation. It is well marked by wooden posts with blue tops and a shoe and horseshoe routed in white under the blue top. Blue paint is used on trees.

Water along much of the trail must be considered unsafe. Boil it or take along purification tablets.

A fire permit is not required. Camping along this trail is permitted. Keep back from streams and lakes. Respect private property.

A backpacker is welcome at any of the ranches along the way. A list of them is available from the addresses below under References.

Location   The Michigan Hiking-Riding Trail is located between the towns of Empire-Elberta on Lake Superior and Tawas City on Lake Huron. Running from west to east, it passes the towns of Kalkaska, Frederick, Grayling, Eldorado, and Luzerne. Spurs reach north from it at Frederick to Johannesburg, Aloha, and Mackinaw City. One spur reaches south to Cadillac, another almost to Midland.

Access   There are many places to join the trail. The western end is popular with horsemen. The eastern end provides more trail in federal lands. There is no way to make a loop hike.

References   The Michigan Trail Riders, Inc., has prepared a booklet that includes among other data detailed county maps showing the location of the trail: $5.00 postpaid. For information on where to purchase this booklet write Michigan Trail Riders, Inc., Chamber of Commerce, Traverse City, Michigan 49684.

For those not wanting to spend the money for the detailed maps, there is a fact sheet put out by the Michigan Department of Natural Resources, Lansing, Michigan 48926. Ask for *Michigan Riding and Hiking Trails*.

PORCUPINE MOUNTAINS STATE PARK

This roadless area provides the hiker with over 58,000 acres of virgin timber, wild rivers, secluded lakes, and rugged mountains. The Porcupine Mountains are thrust-up interbedded sandstone, lava flows, and conglomerates that slope up from Lake Superior in parallel ridges inland from the water. Copper is found in the lava flows capping the ridges that have resisted the ages and elements.

Hundreds of years ago these mountains were given their name because the Chippewas thought they resembled a crouching porcupine. The porcupine still inhabits the area, along with deer, black bear, and coyote.

Only one road penetrates this region to top one of the ridges and overlook Lake of the Clouds. Short spurs off a boundary road provide access to trail heads.

Over eighty miles of trails are designed to give the hiker the best vistas along the routes. There is very fine country to view on every hand.

The trails are in good condition, making for comfortable hiking. However, there are some changes in elevation that will challenge the best backpacker.

Trips of up to a week or more can be easily planned, with a few excellent loop hikes to be made. Any number of day hikes can be taken to fishing spots or secluded scenic areas.

A fire permit is not required. Trailside camping is permitted, but keep a quarter-mile away from any cabin or trail shelter.

The water in the streams is not polluted, but park officials advise boiling water or using purification tablets, especially with lake water.

All trails are well marked with orange or red diamond plates nailed to trees. Junctions are signed.

Season   Spring, summer, and fall.

Location   Porcupine Mountains State Park is located in the western part of Michigan's Upper Peninsula on Lake Superior. State 28 passes south of the park.

Access   At Bergland, State 64 goes north to meet State 107 and the park. The park can be reached by taking a hard-surface road north from Wakefield on State 28.

Transportation Services None to the park. Buses service State 28 to Wakefield and Bergland.

Accommodations Motels and resorts just outside the park on State 107. There are several campgrounds in the park.

Medical Assistance Park first aid. Private assistance in White Pine, Bergland, or Wakefield.

Fishing Trout in the lakes and streams. Bass and perch in Lake of the Clouds. For license information write for *Michigan Fish Laws Digest,* EMTA, Log Office, Bay City, Michigan 48706.

Hunting The park is open during regular seasons. Deer, bear, grouse, and duck are the game. Write for *Game Law Digest,* as above.

References Write for the map-brochure, *Porcupine Mountains State Park,* Park Supervisor, Porcupine Mountains State Park, Route 2, Ontonagon, Michigan 49953.

15-minute quadrangles: Carp River, White Pine, Thomaston, Bergland.

Trip Outlines

Trip A 17 miles, loop hike: 2 days, 1 night
Park car in parking lot at end of State 107. Take Escarpment Trail. This is a cliffside trail overlooking the Porcupine Mountains and the very beautiful Lake of the Clouds. Ascend Cloud Peak. Descend into saddle and climb Cuyahoga Peak. Then down again to reach Government Peak Trail. 4 miles. From this trail take the Overlook Trail, a 3-mile looping route through virgin timber with many fine scenic views. Rejoin Government Peak Trail and continue up Carp River. Pass Union Spring Trail coming from the second largest natural

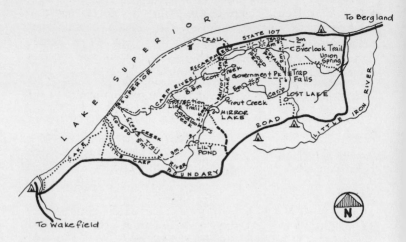

Trail Map for Trips A, B, and C

spring in Michigan: 700 gallons per minute. Pass Trap Falls and make camp. 8½ miles.

Second Day. Pass Lost Lake Trail and ascend Government Peak (1850), second highest point in the park. Descend to reach North Mirror Lake Trail. Turn right here and take this trail down to Scott Creek. Ascend to Escarpment Trail and reach parked car. 8½ miles.

Trip B   24 miles, loop hike: 3 days, 2 nights
Park car in lot at end of State 107. Take North Mirror Lake Trail. Descend to cross outlet from Lake of the Clouds. Cross Scott Creek and start ascending to Mirror Lake. Pass Government Peak Trail on left. Reach Trout Creek and follow along its bank to Mirror Lake. 4 miles. Pass cabins. Pass Correction Line Trail on right. Reach South Mirror Lake Trail on left. Continue on Little Carp River Trail. Reach trail to Lily Pond. Hike to the pond and camp. 7 miles.

Second Day. Retrace steps to Little Carp River Trail and continue on. Reach Little Carp River. Pass falls and cabin. Reach junction of Cross Trail. Take this trail right. Cross Toledo Creek. Pass Big Carp River Trail on right. Continue ahead to Lake Superior. Camp here. 8½ miles.

Third Day. Retrace steps along river to reach junction of Big Carp River Trail on left. Take trail and cross river. Ascend along river to pass Shining Cloud Falls. Cross river. Pass Correction Line Trail. Cross Landlookers Creek. Escarpment is on left. Cross river again and ascend steeply to escarpment. Hike along cliffs to reach parked car. 8½ miles.

Trip C   36 miles, loop hike: 4 days, 3 nights
Start as in Trip A to North Mirror Lake Trail. Then proceed as in Trip B to Lake Superior. Take Lake Superior Trail along shore. Pass cabin and climb to State 107. Hike up road to escarpment and parked car.

Camps can be made at Trap Falls (8½ m.), Lily Pond (9 m.), and Lake Superior (8½ m.).

Observations   This area is worth visiting to hike. Situated as it is, it provides one of the finest backpacking areas in the East. Take along lots of insect repellent in the summer. Be prepared for cold rains also.

TAHQUAMENON FALLS STATE PARK

This state park is in the eastern part of the Upper Peninsula, reaching inland from Whitefish Bay and along the Tahquamenon River. This is Hiawatha's River, and the falls are the largest east of the Mississippi, excepting Niagara Falls. Moose, deer, bear, and wolf still roam through this area.

The main attractions here are the falls, upper and lower. Of interest to a hiker is the trail that winds along the riverbank connecting the falls.

Start from the Lower Falls and take the trail upstream. It is a day trip: 3½-4 hours each way. Carry a lunch.

Access   Take Michigan State 123 north from the Mackinac Bridge to the park.

ISLE ROYALE NATIONAL PARK

A unique backpacking experience awaits those who can afford the trip to Isle Royale. The park is a prime example of wilderness environment, a land of the loon, wolf, and unspoiled scenic beauty. Here one can savor the idea of what it was once like in our nation.

In this 133,000-acre preserve there are 160 miles of trails. Backpacking trips can be planned for up to two weeks. The Greenstone Ridge Trail with side trips to the lakes and bays can take a backpacker a week from Rock Harbor in the north to Windigo at the south end of the island. A flight back to Rock Harbor would make connections for Michigan's Upper Peninsula.

Contact Isle Royale Natural History Association, P.O. Box 27, Houghton, Michigan 49931. Ask for *Wilderness Trails— A Guide to the Trails in Isle Royale,* 50¢. Also write, Superintendent, Isle Royale National Park, 87 North Ripley Street, Houghton, Michigan 49931. Ask for brochure describing park.

SENEY NATIONAL WILDLIFE REFUGE

Located in the Upper Peninsula, this preserve has a 7-mile loop route through its scenic marshes. Over 95,000 acres of pools, marshlands, and small islands support a variety of flora and fauna in a protected environment. Although this route is primarily an auto road, a wonderful experience can be had by taking a day hike. To be seen are nesting islands for Canada geese, bald eagle nests, and a number of smaller birds: flickers, sapsuckers, and pileated woodpeckers. The marshes are feeding grounds for ducks and muskrats. Beavers work here undisturbed. And the wetland shrubs are home for woodcocks and jack snipes.

A visitor center is located near the entry to the preserve. A self-guided tour brochure is available here.

The refuge is located on State 77 just north of Germfask and south of State 28.

CHAPTER 4

TRAILS WEST

COMPRISING THE Rocky Mountain states, this region includes the finest and largest wilderness areas in our nation. Years of hiking are needed to even begin to see the wonders here. Towering peaks rise from forested plateaus. Glacier-fed lakes and streams give birth to the great rivers flowing east and west. And there are the awesome canyons: the Grand Canyon in Arizona, Zion and Canyonlands national parks in Utah. No less a wilderness experience is to be had by visiting the remote grandeur and quiet in the peaks of Arizona's White Mountains, Nevada's spectacular Snake Range rising to 13,000 feet, or Utah's wild and glorious Uinta Range topping that elevation.

At present there is no major trail system such as the Appalachian or Pacific Crest trails. However, many men envisage a Continental Divide Trail following the divide summits from Canada to Mexico. Portions of it exist, maintained by government agencies in their management of the many forest and wilderness areas in this region. When completed, it will surely be the most challenging trail in America.

Longs Peak in Rocky Mountain National Park—
National Park Service photo

WILDERNESS AND PRIMITIVE AREAS

For information on wilderness and primitive areas in the Rocky Mountain West, write the regional headquarters of the USDA Forest Service given below. The wilderness and primitive areas under the jurisdiction of each regional headquarters are listed under the address of that headquarters. (P) stands for primitive area, (W) for wilderness area.

NORTHERN REGION
Federal Building
Missoula, Montana 59801

Absaroka (P)
Anaconda-Pintlar (W)
Beartooth (P)
Bob Marshall (W)
Cabinet Mountains (W)
Gates of the Mountains (W)
Mission Mountains (P)
Salmon River Breaks (P)
Selway-Bitterroot (W)
Spanish Peaks (P)

ROCKY MOUNTAIN REGION
Federal Center Building 85
Denver, Colorado 80225

Cloud Peak (P)
Flat Tops (P)
Glacier (P)
Gore Range-Eagle Nest (P)
La Garita (W)
Maroon Bells-Snowmass (W)
Mt. Zirkel (W)
North Absaroka (W)

Popo Agie (P)
Rawah (W)
San Juan (P)
South Absaroka (W)
Stratified (P)
Uncompahgre (P)
Upper Rio Grande (P)
West Elk (W)
Wilson Mountains (P)

SOUTHWESTERN REGION
Federal Building
517 Gold Avenue SW
Albuquerque, New Mexico 87101

Black Range (P)
Blue Range (P)
Chiricahua (W)
Galiuro (W)
Gila (W & P)
Mazatzal (W)
Mount Baldy (W)
Pecos (W)
Pine Mountain (P)
San Pedro Parks (W)
Sierra Ancha (W)
Superstition (W)
Sycamore Canyon (P)
Wheeler Peak (W)
White Mountain (W)

INTERMOUNTAIN REGION
Federal Office Building
Ogden, Utah 84401

Bridger (W)
High Uintas (P)
Hoover (W)
Idaho (P)
Jarbidge (W)
Sawtooth (P)
Teton (W)

UTAH

CANYONLANDS NATIONAL PARK

This park comprises 258,000 acres where the Green and Colorado rivers meet. Geologically, it is a wonderland of canyons and arches, red sandstone and desert. Among other varied wildlife, the park boasts bighorn sheep and cougar. Hikers on the 84 miles of trails should carry water. There is no fishing in the park. Try to make your visit in the spring or fall.

For map-brochures write Canyonlands National Park, First Western Building, 72 South Main, Moab, Utah 84532.

ZION NATIONAL PARK

A phantasmagoria in sandstone sculptured by the elements, Zion National Park features canyons, mesas, arches, hanging gardens, and waterfalls. Through its 147,000 acres wend 155 miles of trails. The park supports elk, deer, bobcats, and foxes.

Hikers can write for map-brochures to Zion National Park, Springdale, Utah 84767.

ARIZONA

The stellar attraction for outdoor adventurers and photographers in this state is the Grand Canyon, a mile-deep gorge in the Colorado River drainage. The Canyon can be hiked in winter from South Rim, a flat and pine-forested 7,000-foot plateau. North Rim is higher and cooler. Through the 674,000 acres of Grand Canyon National Park snake 239 miles of trails. Fishing is poor.

Write Grand Canyon National Park, P.O. Box 129, Grand Canyon, Arizona 86023 for map-brochures.

NEW MEXICO

Like Colorado above it, New Mexico has the Continental Divide passing through it north to south. At this point the summit elevations lessen and the Divide swings far west to the state's border with Arizona. The Gila Wilderness is here in southwestern New Mexico along with the Black Range Wilderness.

High country is found in the northeast above Santa Fe, where the great range of the Sangre de Cristo Mountains reaches down from Colorado with peaks topping 13,000 feet. This outstanding hike country provides the backpacker with endless opportunities to get away from it all. Of prime interest is the Pecos Wilderness Area.

PECOS WILDERNESS

Here in the Sangre de Cristo Mountains 165,000 acres of high country has been set aside. Lofty peaks, lakes, alpine meadows, and deep forests characterize this region. Snowbound much of the year, this land of unsurpassed vistas is an important watershed for the area. More than 400 creeks give birth to the Pecos River.

Forests of spruce, fir, and aspen grow in the valleys and atop the broad mesas.

Deer, black bear, and elk are in the forests. Look for beaver at higher altitudes, wild turkey in the ponderosa pine zone.

Season   Spring, summer, and fall. July and August is the rainy season here. Excellent backpacking here in the latter part of August and September.

Location   Pecos Wilderness Area is located in north-central New Mexico just east of Santa Fe.

Access   State 3 passes on its eastern and northern border. Interstate 25 passes south of the area, while U.S. 285 and State 76 pass its western border. Other roads lead in close to the area from these highways.

Transportation Services   Bus to Pecos on southern border. Bus to Santa Fe and Las Vegas.

Accommodations   Hotels, motels, resorts in Santa Fe and Las Vegas and along the highways of the west, south and east borders. Campgrounds surround the area.

Medical Assistance   Santa Fe or Las Vegas.

Fishing   Trout in the streams and lakes. Buy a license locally or write New Mexico Department of Fish and Game, Santa Fe, New Mexico 87501.

Hunting   Good for deer, bear, elk, and turkey. For seasons, game, and licenses write as above.

Recreation   A visit to Santa Fe must be included in any trip to this region. It is a charming town, the seat of state government, with many historic buildings and places of interest. The Palace of the Governors was built in 1610. In the vicinity are a number of pueblos, some active and others now in ruins or partially restored.

An hour drive south of Santa Fe is Albuquerque and massive Sandia Mountain with its aerial train. Atop the peak one can watch jet liners fly in below to land at the city.

Wilderness Trails   Any kind of hike can be planned for this area—a day's hike or two-week outing. Many miles of trails have been developed for the benefit of hikers and sportsmen. For the most part, the trails start above 8,000 feet. Much of the trail system is in open forest, alpine meadows, or above timberline at elevations like 11,000 feet or better.

The trails are in good condition and signed.

Permits are not required. Camp can be made anywhere.

Water is plentiful.

References   Write for map-brochure, *Pecos Wilderness,* District Ranger, Pecos Ranger Station, Pecos, New Mexico 87552. Also ask for map-brochure of Santa Fe and Carson national forests.

7½-minute quadrangles: Cowles, Elk Mountain, Pecos Falls, Truchas Peak.

Write for the very fine and authoritative book, *Trail Guide to the Upper Pecos,* Villagra Book Shop, P.O. Box 460, Santa Fe, New Mexico 87501. $1.75 postpaid.

Trip Outlines

Trip A   22 miles, loop hike: 3 days, 2 nights
Base at Iron Gate Campground (9400), 4 miles north of F.S. Road 223 after it leaves State 63 about one mile south of Cowles.

Start hike by climbing through evergreen forest on F.S. Trail 249. Pass F.S. Trail 250 on right and leading down to Mora Flats. Continue ahead on narrow ridge. Mora Canyon on right, and Pecos River on left. Reach grassy meadows atop Hamilton Mesa. Fine views of Truchas Peaks from here; Santa Barbara Divide to the distant north. To the west is Pecos Baldy Summit (12500). Pass trail on left descending to Beatty's Cabins. Continue ahead across open meadows above 10,000 feet. More fine views. Reach trail junction. Trail to left leads to Beatty's and Pecos River. To the right

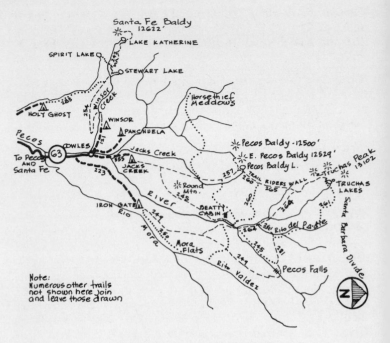

Trail Map for Trips A, B, and C

is the Rio Valdez. Good lunch stop after 6 miles of comfortable hiking.

Continue ahead alternately through open meadows and forest. The sound of Pecos Falls will be heard on left. Reach trail junction (10600). Keep left and descend to Pecos River and Falls (10400). Camp here. 10 miles.

Second Day. Hike west up and away from the falls to reach F.S. Trail 245. Continue left on F.S. Trail 245 a short distance; then take F.S. Trail 281 right. Climb out of Jarosa

Canyon. Cross ridge (10900) and descend to Rito del Padre and F.S. Trail 261 (10100). Hike downstream via F.S. Trails 261 and 264 to reach Beatty's Cabins (9600). Camp here. 5 miles.

Third Day. Cross over to east bank of Pecos River and take the most southern trail to hike out of Pecos River valley and up to Hamilton Mesa. Reach trail of first day (F.S. Trail 249) and hike back down to Iron Gate Campground. 7 miles.

Observations   This is a very easy hike. The first day, although long in mileage, has very little climbing.

Trip B   18 miles, return trip: 3 days, 2 nights
Base at Winsor Creek Campground (8400) about one mile west of Cowles on F.S. Road 121. Take trail east from campground along north bank of Winsor Creek. Cross creek and within a few hundred feet reach abandoned trail continuing along creek. Main trail turns back here to climb east up to ridge (9400) overlooking Cowles and Pecos Valley. It then swings back west along ridge. Pass trail from Holy Ghost Campground. Pass junction of old abandoned trail coming up from Winsor Creek. Cross gully. Reach trail from Stewart Lake (10200). Good lunch stop. Continue on and ascend via switchbacks. Pass trail on left to Spirit Lake. Ascend steeply up boulder ridge. Trail becomes open as it climbs through granite boulder field. Top ridge and descend to edge of Lake Katherine (11700) set below the 1,000-foot granite walls of Santa Fe Baldy. Camp here. 9 miles.

Second Day. Climb to summit of Santa Fe Baldy (12600). From the north side of the lake climb to a ridge that runs west to join the main summit ridge running south to the peak. Magnificent views here of the entire region.

Third Day. Return via first day routes. 9 miles.

Trip C   31 miles, loop hike: 5 days, 4 nights
Base at Jack's Creek Campground (8900) north of Cowles
by 2½ miles on F.S. Road 555. Take trail north for
Beatty's Cabin and Pecos Baldy Lake. Climb steeply along
Round Mountain ridge overlooking Jack's Creek. Reach
narrow ridge (10000). After 4 miles reach trail junction.
Trail to right leads to Beatty's Cabin. Keep left and hike
through broad meadows. Descend to Jack's Creek. Pass
trail on left to Horsethief Meadows. Hike in open meadows
and aspen groves. Pass trail on right to Beatty's Cabin. Ascend through forest. Reach open country. Reach Pecos Baldy
Lake (11500) nestled below East Pecos Baldy (12529).
Camp here. 9 miles.

Second Day. Climb to summit of East Pecos Baldy. A trail
leads up the southern face. Trail leaves main trail a few
hundred feet south of lake.

Third Day. Leave lake and ascend north to hike below Trail
Riders Wall (Truchas Divide) via F.S. Trails 260, 265, and
264. Pass under Truchas Peak and reach Truchas Lakes
(11870). Camp here. 5 miles.

Fourth Day. Leave Truchas Lakes and retrace steps to descend via F.S. Trail 264 to Beatty's Cabin. Camp here. 7
miles.

Fifth Day. Take F.S. Trail 245 east of Round Mountain
along the ridge and down to Jack's Creek Campground. 10
miles.

COLORADO

More than any other state, this one provides more of what is
considered "ideal" for hikers and backpackers. High
country is the feature that draws so many here to hike atop

snowcapped mountains and forested plateaus. Many trails start above 8,000 feet, an elevation higher than that reached by most of the trails in America.

Of principal interest are the wild and rugged ranges running north-south in the center of Colorado, the Continental Divide, the scattered ranges to the west, and the plateau-canyon country on its far western border with Utah. Even here much of the region remains above 6,000 feet.

Summer weather is cool at these elevations, and in this respect hiking is a real pleasure. However, typical of much of the state are late afternoon thunderstorms amongst the peaks. Frosty mornings are not unusual, nor are blizzards at high altitudes. Offsetting this is the magnificence of soaring peaks, alpine meadows splashed with color, the sightings of great elk herds, bands of sheep, and the savoring of trout from unequaled fishing streams.

ROCKY MOUNTAIN NATIONAL PARK

Rare alpine beauty is the feature of this park. Its 410 square miles of high-altitude valleys, lakes and streams, flowered meadows, and snowcapped mountains topping 14,000 feet are becoming a favorite area for hikers and backpackers. The Continental Divide passes through the park along the Front Range of the Rocky Mountains. Forests and plateaus are home for black bear, deer, elk, and bighorn sheep. The golden eagle is seen in the skies over these mountains.

Season   July through September. Do not hike until after July 15 to be sure of high-country trails.

Location   The Rocky Mountain National Park is located in north-central Colorado northwest of Denver.

Access   U.S. 34 passes through the park. Interstate 25 (north-south) brings traffic to its eastern border.

Transportation Services   Bus service on U.S. 34 to Grand Lake and Estes Park.

Accommodations   Motels, resorts, lodges at Estes Park on east side of park and Grand Lake on west side. Campgrounds within the park and surrounding national forests.

Medical Assistance   Park first aid. Private assistance in Estes Park and Grand Lake.

Fishing   Excellent for trout in the streams and lakes. Colorado license needed. Buy one locally or write Division of Game, Fish and Parks, 6060 Broadway, Denver, Colorado 80216.

Hunting   None.

Recreation   Denver is only 2 hours' drive from the park. A visit there might include a look at the U.S. Mint and the Colorado State Museum.

To the west is the ride up Mt. Evans on the highest auto road in the United States. Mt. Evans is 14,264 feet high. Also in this area is Lookout Mountain and the grave of Buffalo Bill Cody with a small museum.

Just west of Denver is Red Rock Park with its outdoor theater set amongst great sandstone formations.

Park Trails   Over 300 miles of trails have been developed in the park. Hikers can take leisurely strolls along interpretive walks, move into the backcountry for a week or more, or set their sights on a mountain peak.

All the trails are in good condition and signed.

Water is plentiful.

Permits are required. Camp only at designated areas or ask Rangers about alternate campsites.

References   Write for map-brochure of the park to Rocky Mountain Nature Association, Estes Park, Colorado 80517.

Also ask for 27 x 26 minute topographical map of the park.
$1.15 postpaid.

7½-minute quadrangles: McHenry Peak, Grand Lake,
Fall River Pass for trails described.

Trip Outlines

Trip A   30½ miles, loop hike: 4 days, 3 nights
Start on the west side of the park at Grand Lake. On the north
side of town, along State 278 to the West Portal of the cross-
mountain water tunnel, there is parking at roadside. Look for
signs.

Take dirt road up to where trail starts (8520) on left at sharp
right turn in road. Hike on the western side of Tonahutu Creek.

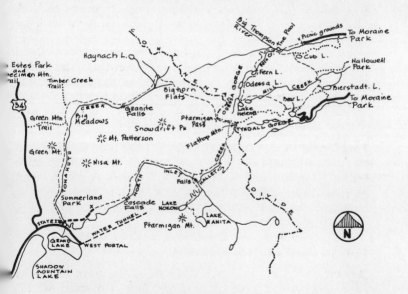

Trail Map for Trips A and C

This is a very pleasant hike along a valley between Green Mountain and Nisa Mountain. Reach Big Meadows (9400). Pass Green Mountain Trail on left. Skirt Big Meadows. Pass Timber Creek Trail on left. Leave meadow and continue up Tonahutu Creek to reach Granite Falls (9800). Continue on to make camp above falls about 1 mile. 8½ miles.

Second Day. Ascend to meet Haynach Lakes outlet and Tonahutu Creek forks. Views south to Mt. Patterson (11424) and the broad plateau reaching east to Snowdrift Peak (12274) may yield sighting of elk herds. Cross creek in rocky open area (10600). Start steep climb, leaving treeline and reaching Big Horn Flats. Top-of-the-world views here to the snowy Never Summer Mountains and the Mummy Range. The plateau is a carpet of flowers watered by lingering snowbanks. A good lunch stop.

Continue on to Ptarmigan Pass (12200). Wonderful views east into Odessa Gorge. Pass trail on right. Continue up to Flattop Mountain (12324) and junction with trail from Bear Lake. Views into Tyndall Gorge. Turn right and descend to join North Inlet Trail across plateau and into Hallet Creek drainage via switchbacks. Cross Hallet Creek and reach camp (10520). 9 miles.

Third Day. Descend along Hallet Creek via switchbacks to North Inlet (9600). Reach trail on left to Lakes Nokoni and Nanita. Take this and ascend steeply via switchbacks to Lake Nokoni (10800). Camp here or climb another three-fourths mile to Lake Nanita. Either place provides excellent fishing and good camping. 4 miles.

Fourth Day. Descend from lakes to North Inlet Trail and continue on down very pleasant route. Pass Cascade Falls. Reach Summerland Park and road end (another car could be parked here). Take road out to parked car. 9 miles.

Observations   This is a very easy trail for the most part. Stiff hiking on second and third mornings only. Incredible scenery at summits.

Trip B   6 miles, return hike: 1 day (not shown on map)
A delightful but vigorous day hike leads to top of Specimen Mountain (12489), one of the highest trails in the park. The trail starts at a parking lot on the northwest shore of Poudre Lake (10750). Start steep climb and soon reach open fields and the Continental Divide. Trail goes up hard on ridge and Divide. Can be very windy and chilly here. All horizons visible. At the top there is a metal cylinder with a scroll to add your name. Take a lunch and, when descending, break away from the trail into the trees and a secluded lunch spot.

Trip C   17 miles, loop hike: 3 days, 2 nights
Start at the end of Moraine Park Road (8200). Take Fern Lake Trail along easy grade to The Pool. Cross Big Thompson River. Trail to Cub Lake on left. Start steep climb to Fern Lake (9520). Continue on climbing alongside Fern Creek to Odessa Lake (10000). Camp here. 5 miles.

Second Day. Leave Odessa Lake and hike out of Odessa Gorge to pass near Lake Helene (10560), Two Rivers Lake, and Marigold Pond. Descend to cross Mill Creek and skirt base of Flattop Mountain to reach Flattop Mountain Trail on right. Pass trail from Bear Lake on right. Continue on down and take trail on right to Bierstadt Lake (9416). Camp here. 6 miles.

Third Day. Rejoin trail leading into Mill Creek Basin. Pass trail from Hallowell Park along Mill Creek. Cross Mill Creek (9000) and climb from basin to ridge (9400). Descend to reach trail on right to Cub Lake. Keep left on trail descending to The Pool and Fern Lake Trail. Take this trail back down to parked car. 6 miles.

LA GARITA WILDERNESS

Astride the Continental Divide, the 49,000 acres of this Wilderness is part of the Gunnison and Rio Grande national forests. Its name comes from Spanish, meaning "The Overlook." Alpine scenery, rugged terrain, beautiful flowered meadows, full rushing streams, and peaks reaching better than 14,000 feet are here for those seeking a very special wilderness experience.

These mountains are a natural habitat for black bear and mountain lion. Elk, deer, and bighorn sheep climb into this area to summer. Fishing is good in all the streams.

At present this Wilderness enjoys a certain amount of real solitude. It has not been "discovered" as have so many of this nation's wilderness areas.

Season Mid-June through September. Hike after July 1 to be sure high country trails are open.

Location La Garita Wilderness is located in south-central Colorado west of Saguache and south of Gunnison.

Access State 114 passes on the northern border of the Wilderness, and State 149 reaches in close to the southern border. Dirt roads reach the area's boundary from State 114.

Transportation Services None.

Accommodations Motels in Saguache. Campgrounds surround the wilderness area.

Medical Assistance Gunnison.

Fishing Native and eastern brook trout. Big ones in Machin Lake. Buy a Colorado license locally or write Department of Game, Fish and Parks, 6060 Broadway, Denver, Colorado 80216.

Hunting Bear, deer, elk, mountain lion. For seasons, licenses, etc., write as above.

Recreation Northwest of the Wilderness is the Curecanti National Recreation Area with its Blue Mesa Lake and dams. Water sports are the main pastime here. A little further west is the Black Canyon of the Gunnison, a deep rugged gorge that seldom sees sunlight.

To the north is Mt. Elbert (14431), the highest point in Colorado. Nearby is Leadville and its mine-pocked hills. This boom town has not changed much. Some of the old houses and mines have been preserved.

East from the Wilderness is the Great Sand Dunes National Monument, 1,000-foot-deep sand dunes pushed up against the Sangre de Cristo Mountains.

Wilderness Trails This is not a large wilderness area, but there are many miles of good trails well signed. This is all high-country hiking, much of it above 9,000 feet. Trails generally follow drainages in the shadow of snow-patched summits. Ridge trails provide excellent views of the great peaks in the area.

Water is plentiful.

Permits are not required. Camp may be made anywhere, but use established sites whenever possible.

Before a trip write or visit District Ranger, Saguache Ranger Station, Saguache, Colorado 81149 for the latest information on trails.

References Write for map-brochure of La Garita Wilderness and Rio Grande National Forest, District Ranger, Saguache Ranger Station, Saguache, Colorado 81149.

7½-minute quadrangles: Mesa Mountain, Saguache Park, Elk Park.

15-minute quadrangle: Creede.

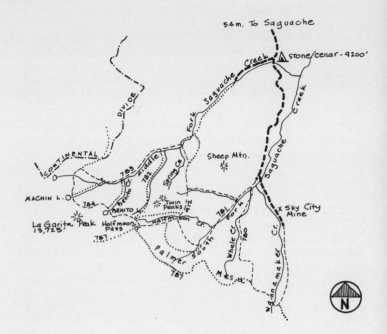

Trail Map for Trips A and B

Trip Outlines

Trip A   11½ miles, loop hike: 2 days, 1 night
From Saguache take State 114 22 miles west to F.S. Road 750. Then proceed 18 miles to Stone Cellar Campground (9200). Another 7 miles on F.S. Road 787 leads to parking and trail head. Another road continues on across creek and up to Sky City Mine and a little beyond. Caution: be sure you have enough gasoline to return the 60 miles to Saguache.

At trail head hike into Wilderness on F.S. Trail 780 crossing South Fork Saguache Creek and following Whale

Creek. Leave Whale Creek and climb to Palmer Mesa and junction with F.S. Trail 787, the Stock Driveway. Take this trail left to junction with trail down Wannamaker Creek to Sky City Mine. Camp here. 6½ miles.

Second Day. Descend to pass Sky City Mine and reach parked car. 5 miles.

Trip B 29½ miles, loop hike: 4 days, 3 nights
Start as above, but remain on F.S. Trail 781 up South Fork Saguache Creek. Pass Halfmoon Creek on right. Reach trail on right leading up to Halfmoon Creek and F.S. Trail 912. Camp here. 7½ miles.

Second Day. Take F.S. Trail 912 west and up Halfmoon Creek to Halfmoon Pass (12500) and junction with F.S. Trail 787 (Stock Driveway). From the pass are excellent views of the surrounding country. From pass hike north on F.S. Trail 784 leading to Machin Lake. Pass F.S. Trail 782 leading down North Twin Peaks Creek. Descend to Benito Lake and reach Machin Lake. Camp here. 7 miles.

Third Day. Leave Machin Lake to cross Middle Creek and reach junction with F.S. Trail 783. Take this trail down to Middle Creek. Pass Benito Creek junction. Leave Wilderness boundary. Pass junction with F.S. Trail 782 and reach Spring Creek. Camp here. 8 miles.

Fourth Day. Hike up Spring Creek to reach F.S. Trail 912. Continue on F.S. Trail 912 to junction with trail to South Fork Saguache Creek and F.S. Trail 781. Hike down this trail to wilderness boundary and parking. 7 miles.

SAN JUAN PRIMITIVE AREA

Now under consideration for wilderness classification, this 230,000-acre preserve is one of the nation's largest. It is all high country, averaging over 10,000 feet. Scores of peaks top 13,000 feet, while three reach more than 14,000 feet.

Like other alpine regions in our nation, glaciers have sculptured valleys and canyons here. Beautiful alpine meadows and forests contrast pleasantly with rugged granitic extrusions, rocky barren areas, and lingering snow packs.

Fir, pine, and spruce cover the mountain slopes. Open areas are dressed with shrubs and grasses. Wild flowers bloom from spring to late autumn at lower elevations, while at alpine levels they have a brief few weeks of splendid color.

The watchful hiker might glimpse elk, deer, bighorn sheep, or even black bear. Chances are that coyotes will be heard during the night. The mountains are also home for smaller mammals: rabbits, badgers, bobcats, and beavers. In the streams and lakes trout await the angler.

Season   Mid-July through mid-September.

Location   The San Juan Primitive Area is located in southwest Colorado, north of Durango.

Access   U.S. 160 passes south of the Primitive Area, while U.S. 550 passes its western border. Dirt roads reach close to the area's northern and western boundary. Access is best on dirt roads coming to the area from the south and U.S. 160.

Transportation Services   Bus service on U.S. 160 and U.S. 550.

Accommodations   Motels, hotels, resorts in Durango, Silverton, and along U.S. 160 and U.S. 550. Campgrounds surround the area.

Medical Assistance   Durango and Silverton.

Fishing   Trout in streams and lakes. Buy Colorado license locally or write Division of Game, Fish and Parks, 6060 Broadway, Denver, Colorado 80216.

Hunting   Bear, elk, bighorn sheep, mountain lion. For all game, licenses, seasons etc., write as above.

Recreation   Of real interest to any hiker reaching this area will be Mesa Verde National Park west of the Primitive Area. Exploring the mesa-top pit houses, pueblos, and cliff dwellings is an exciting experience. There are some fine short hikes to be taken here.

Wilderness Trails   Over 240 miles of trails have been constructed in this region. Some of these had their beginnings with the animals and Indians. Spanish explorers came to the area in 1765 and 1776. The Americans, Pike, Gilpen, and Frémont, followed from 1807 through 1849, leading the vanguard of pioneers and gold searchers. Before them trappers and hunters had already worked through the mountains. Today there is a fine network of trails developed by the Forest Service.

Most of the trails are in good condition and signed.

Water is plentiful.

Permits are not required. Campsites can be made anywhere. Try to use established sites or designated areas.

This is an area well suited to casual day hikes or overnighters. However, it is a high-use area, something to be expected in light of the spectacular country. If possible, plan trips for midweek.

References   Write for map-brochure, *San Juan Primitive Area*, District Ranger, Pine Ranger Station, Bayfield, Colorado 81122. Also ask for map-brochure of San Juan National Forest.

15-minute quadrangle: Needles Mountains for Trip A.

7½-minute quadrangle: Granite Peak for first part of Trips B and C. No maps available for remainder of trip.

Trip Outlines

Trip A   30½ miles, loop hike: 4 days, 3 nights
A unique trip can be had for the price of a railway ticket. A narrow-gauge train runs north between Durango and Silverton along the western border of the primitive area. It leaves early morning and returns in the evening.

Take the train to Needleton. From there cross the Animas River and take the trail up Needle Creek to Chicago Basin. Camp here. 7½ miles.

Second Day. Ascend to Columbine Pass (12500) and descend along Johnson Creek to Vallecito Creek. Turn upstream and reach junction of Rock Creek and Vallecito Creek. Camp here. 9 miles.

Third Day. Ascend to Hunchback Pass and hike trail to Elk Creek. Camp here. 7 miles.

Fourth Day. Descend Elk Creek to Elk Park and railroad to Durango. 7 miles.

Observations   Check train schedules. Plan on spending a night camped at Elk Park if the train is missed. You must flag it as it approaches.

For information about the train schedules and tickets write to Agent, Rio Grande Depot, Durango, Colorado 81301.

Trip B   30 miles, return trip: 4 days, 3 nights
From U.S. 160 at Bayfield east of Durango take road north about 22 miles, passing Vallecito Lake's east shore and reaching Pine River Campground. With an early morning start, hike to Emerald Lake and camp at south end. 9 miles.

Second Day. Hike around lake to Lake Creek and ascend to Moon Lakes. Camp Here. 6 miles.

Third Day. Return to Emerald Lake. 6 miles.

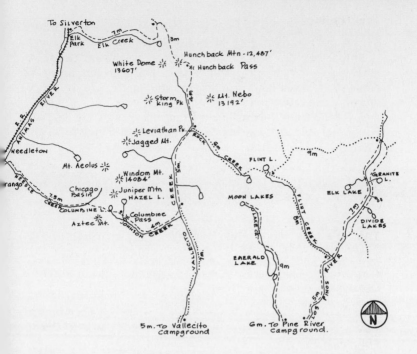

To Silverton
Elk Park
Elk Creek 7m 3m
Hunchback Mtn - 12,487'
White Dome 13607' Hunchback Pass
E.Z. ANIMAS RIVER
Storm King Pk Mt. Nebo 13192'
Leviathan Pk.
Jagged Mt.
ROCK CREEK 6m
FLINT L. 9m
GRANITE L.
Needleton
Mt. Aeolus
Windom Mt 14084'
Juniper Mtn HAZEL L.
MOON LAKES
ELK LAKE 7m
DIVIDE LAKES
rango CREEK 7.5m COLUMBINE L.
Chicago Basin
Columbine Pass
Aztec Mt. JOHNSON CREEK 4m
VALLECITO CREEK
EMERALD LAKE 9m
FLINT CREEK 6m
LAKE 6 9m
LOS PINOS RIVER 5m
5m. To Vallecito campground
6m. To Pine River Campground.
N

Trail Map for Trips A, B, and C

Fourth Day. Return to Pine River Campground. 9 miles.

Trip C   37 miles, return hike: 5 days, 4 nights
Start as above, but continue on trail up Los Pinos River to established campground just inside Primitive Area. Camp here. 7 miles.

Second Day. Continue up Los Pinos River. Pass Flint Creek junction. Cross to east side of river and reach Divide Lakes. Camp here. 8 miles.

Third Day. Continue up Los Pinos River drainage. Pass under Granite Lake. Rejoin trail on west side of Los Pinos River and return downstream to Elk Lake outlet creek. Camp here. 7 miles.

Fourth Day. Continue down Los Pinos River to camps inside Primitive Area. 8 miles.

Fifth Day. Return to Pine River Campground. 7 miles.

WYOMING

The Continental Divide from northwestern to south-central Wyoming, where it continues into Colorado, provides the hiker with some of the most rugged country in America, with peaks over 13,000 feet and trails to reach them.

Yellowstone National Park, along with several wilderness areas and forests, straddles the divide in the northwest. In the southwest there is the Red Desert Country of Rock Springs, Kemmerer, the Flaming Gorge Reservoir, and the Overland Trail Route leading to Utah. In the east the mass of the Bighorn Range rises more than 13,000 feet out of the plains. In the southeast the Snowy Range, a rugged remote area of heavily timbered mountains, rises 12,000 feet. It is usually snow-patched through summer.

GRAND TETON NATIONAL PARK

This park is a land of two extremes. Lofty peaks of gray rock 2.5 billion years old rise abruptly from the glacier basin of lakes and sagebrush flats known as Jackson Hole. No sight is more impressive than to approach the gray wall of pinnacles and crags from the east, overlooking reflecting Jackson Lake.

The Grand Teton (13770) is the major peak amongst a line of mountains topping 12,000 feet. Pine, fir, spruce, cottonwood, and aspen cover the slopes and glaciated canyons. Wild, plunging streams carry off snowmelt from perpetual snows lodged in rocky cirques beneath the peaks. The valleys and alpine mountain slopes are carpeted with wild flowers in summer.

The park provides sanctuary for antelope, elk, moose, deer, and black bear. A variety of birds are to be seen, and the streams and lakes harbor trout for the angler.

Season　July through October. After July 15 for high-country trails.

Location　Grand Teton National Park is located in northwestern Wyoming, just south of Yellowstone National Park.

Access　The park is easily reached by many major highways. U.S. 26, 89, and 187 course into the park from the south, U.S. 26 from the east and west. Interstate 90 (east-west) passes to the north, while Interstate 80 and 80N pass to the south and west respectively.

Transportation Services　Bus service and airlines to Jackson.

Accommodations　Hotels, motels, resorts in Jackson. Lodges in the park. Campgrounds in the park and surrounding national forests.

Medical Assistance　Park first aid. Private assistance in Jackson.

Fishing　Fish the lakes and streams for trout. A Wyoming state license is needed. Buy one locally or write Wyoming Game and Fish Commission, Box 1589, Cheyenne, Wyoming 82001.

Hunting　None.

Recreation Nearby Jackson is a vacationer's town. Good restaurants, accommodations, shops, and theaters make this a very pleasant stop on any trip.

Teton Village west of Jackson is a wonderful stopover with all the amenities. An aerial tram takes you to the top of Rendezvous Mountain for $3.00—an exciting trip with great views of Jackson Hole and the surrounding mountains. Stay up there all day and hike out across the ridges. Take skis and try a run on summer snows.

Mountain climbing classes are based in Jackson and Teton Village. Or try one of the float trips down the Snake River.

To the north is Yellowstone National Park.

Park Trails There are over 200 miles of trails here, all of them well maintained. A variety of hikes can be planned. It is as well suited to a day hike as it is to a week's outing. Many loop hikes are possible. And no matter the length of the trip, one is assured of superb and exciting views of the peaks.

The trail heads and junctions are signed.

Water is plentiful.

A fire-camping permit is required. Use designated campsites whenever possible. There are enough situated at comfortable intervals. Some campsites prohibit use of firewood. Carry a stove.

References Write for map-brochure of park to Grand Teton Natural History Association, Grand Teton National Park, Moose, Wyoming 83012. Also ask for topographic map of Grand Teton National Park. $1.65 postpaid. An excellent guidebook can be had from same address: *Teton Trails,* $1.15 postpaid.

Trip Outlines

Trip A 38 miles, one way: 5 days, 4 nights
From Teton Village west of Jackson, take the aerial tram to

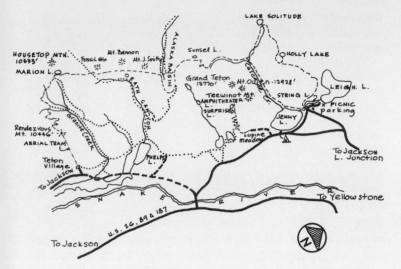

Trail Map for Trips A, B, and C

Rendezvous Mountain (10446). Wonderful views looking to all points of the compass. Descend sharply to pass cirque on left and round ridge for easier descent to South Fork Granite Creek. Continue down to reach trail on left to Middle Fork Granite Creek and ascend to Skyline Trail. Turn right on Skyline Trail. Climb out of Middle Fork Basin, reach small plateau (9300) and descend to North Fork Granite Creek. Ascend steeply to Marion Lake (9240). Camp here. 9 miles.

Second Day. Hike out of Marion Lake and cross divide (9550). Pass under Spearhead Peak (10129) and reach divide again, at head of Death Canyon. Take Death Canyon Shelf Trail to Alaska Basin. This trail follows a prominent bench below Fossil, Bannon, and Jedediah Smith mountains, all nearly 11,000 feet. Wonderful views into Death Canyon. Reach a broad plateau under Mt. Meek. Cross divide (9750) and descend into Alaska Basin, passing Teton Creek and reaching campsites at Basin Lakes (9550). Camp here. 8 miles.

Third Day. Climb out of Alaska Basin. Top divide (10000) and descend to pass Sunset Lake (9608). Start steep climb to Hurricane Pass (10372). Reach the pass. Excellent views of the three Tetons and matchless scenic beauty. Descend via switchbacks to trail on right leading to Avalanche Divide (10600). Notice the limestone of The Wall on right and Schoolroom Glacier. The small lake at this glacier's front has a cloudy appearance caused by fine rock powder from the glacial action. Views of the Tetons are magnificent from this point. Continue to descend along South Fork Cascade Creek. Enter treeline and pass through the world's largest known whitebark pines and green meadows ablaze with color in July and August. Camp here at designated sites. 6 miles.

Fourth Day. Reach junction with Cascade Canyon Trail leading down to Jenny Lake and trail to Lake Solitude. Start climb to Lake Solitude. The forest of spruce and fir is left behind as the trail ascends through talus slopes and meadows. Backward glances overlook Grand Teton (13766), Mt. Owen (12922) and Teewinot Mountain (12317). You are hiking on a perfect example of glacial carving. The great glaciers of the ice ages wore away the once V-shaped rocky canyon walls to leave U-shaped basins with steep, smooth walls. Reach the moraine damming Lake Solitude (9035). On the north are the best campsites. Camp here. 5 miles.

Fifth Day. Ascend to Paintbrush Divide (10650) via switchbacks. Outstanding views from here. Descend from this divide down series of glacial stairsteps with their beautiful meadows and steep descents to the next step. Wild flowers are the feature of the hike down Paintbrush Canyon to String Lake. Reach String Lake (6870) and parking. 10 miles.

Trip B   20 miles, loop hike: 3 days, 2 nights
Start at String Lake parking area at String Lake Outlet. Take trail to Hidden Falls, passing along northwest side of Jenny Lake (6779). Climb to Hidden Falls, Inspiration Point, and magnificent views of Jenny Lake and Jackson Hole. Reach Cascade Forks (7725) and take trail to Lake Solitude. About a half-mile up the trail reach campsite. 7 miles.

Second Day. Ascend to Lake Solitude (9035) and over Paintbrush Divide (10650). Descend Paintbrush Canyon and reach trail to Holly Lake. Camp at Holly Lake (9410). 6½ miles.

Third Day. Return to Paintbrush Canyon Trail and descend to parking at String Lake. 6½ miles.

Trip C   10 miles, return trip: 2 days, 1 night
Leave the Teton Park Road just south of Jenny Lake and cross Cottonwood Creek Bridge to Lupine Meadows parking area. Take trail to Amphitheater Lake, a series of switchbacks up the lower eastern slopes of the Grand Teton. Wonderful vistas on this hike. This is about a 3,000-foot ascent, passing Surprise Lake (9540) and reaching Amphitheater (9698) in the cirque basin just east of Disappointment Peak (11616). Camp here. 5 miles.

Second Day. Return to parking.

YELLOWSTONE NATIONAL PARK

Just north of Grand Teton National Park is Yellowstone National Park. Comprising 2,222,000 acres, it is one of our largest parks. Blessed with magnificent scenery—geysers, hot springs, waterfalls, canyons, and petrified trees—Yellowstone National Park is a wildlife refuge which boasts good fishing and 1,100 miles of trails.

Hikers may obtain map-brochures of the park by writing to Yellowstone National Park, Wyoming 82190.

BIGHORN NATIONAL FOREST

This national forest comprises 1,121,541 acres of land astride the Bighorn Mountains, a unique range that rises abruptly from the Great Plains. Named by the Indians, in reference to thousands of bighorn sheep that once grazed at the Bighorn River and on the mountains, this area is a splendid land for hikers.

History has left its mark on the region. The mountains were a venerable place to the Indians. The mysterious Medicine Wheel remains unexplained to this day. Lewis and Clark came through here in 1805. And in this region the Sioux, Crow, and Cheyenne, trying to resist the advances of white men, were finally crushed after many bloody battles.

Today this forest is a favorite place of outdoorsmen who know this special out-of-the-way wilderness. Located as it is, it is not plagued by the crowds of the more popular western forests and parks along the Continental Divide.

CLOUD PEAK PRIMITIVE AREA

This comprises 92,000 acres in the most rugged part of the Bighorn Range. Hikers will find the very best in wilderness travel here. All of the region is high country ranging from 8,500 feet to over 13,000 feet. Deer, elk, moose, and sheep are to be sighted on the trails. Trout fishing ranks with the best in America.

Season July through September.

Location The Bighorn National Forest is located in north-central Wyoming on the Montana border.

Access   U.S. 14 passes through the forest in the north, while U.S. 16 passes through it in the south. Interstate 90 and U.S. 87 parallel its eastern border.

Transportation Services   Bus service on U.S. 14, 16, and 87.

Accommodations   Hotels, motels in Buffalo and Sheridan. Public and private campgrounds surround the area.

Medical Assistance   Buffalo and Sheridan.

Fishing   Some of the best trout fishing in America. Buy a license locally or write Wyoming Game and Fish Commission, Box 1589, Chyenne, Wyoming 82001.

Hunting   Excellent for deer, elk, bighorn sheep, bear, moose, and antelope. For license, game, season write above address.

Recreation   Rich in Indian wars history, this area has several historic sites commemorating the last futile attempts of the Indians to remain free.

To the west in Cody are the very fine Whitney Gallery of Western Art and Buffalo Bill Museum. There are no better places than these depicting western lore.

Southwest of the area is Thermopolis, site of the world's largest mineral hot springs. From this spring 18,600,000 gallons of water at 135 degrees Fahrenheit flow daily.

Driving east, vacationers can include a visit to the remarkable Devil's Tower National Monument. It rises 865 feet from the plains, a pier of fluted rock that was a landmark for explorers and a mysterious place for the Indians.

Wilderness Trails   Within the Cloud Peak Primitive Area many miles of trails have been developed for outdoorsmen, most of them above 8,500 feet and climbing to countless lakes and summits.

The trails are in good condition and signed.

Water is plentiful.

No permits are required. Camp can be made anywhere, but please try to use established sites.

References Write for the map-brochure, *Bighorn National Forest,* District Ranger, Paintrock Ranger Station, Greybull, Wyoming 82426. Ask for the Forest Service trail map of the Cloud Peak Primitive Area.

7½-minute quadrangles: Shell Lake, Lake Solitude, Spanish Point, Cloud Peak

Trip Outlines

Trip A 22 miles, return hike: 2 days, 1 night
East of Shell take U.S. 14 16 miles to F.S. Road 610 on right and then head southeast. Pass Shell Creek Ranger Station and drive another 18 miles to base at either Upper Paint Rock or Upper Medicine Lodge Lake campgrounds. Trail starts just east of Paint Rock Lakes Guard Station (9200).

Take F.S. Trail 59 south on very easy trail to Lower Paint Rock Lake (9174). Bear east and ascend gradually to top rise above Sheep Creek. Cross creek and head for Teepee Pole Flats. Descend to reach the flats and North Paintrock Creek. Reach junction with F.S. Trail 38 leading left to Lake Geneva and Cliff Lake, leading right to Lake Solitude. Bear right and ascend from creek to pass Poacher Lake (9700). Descend gradually to Paintrock Creek. Pass trail on right to Hyatt Cow Camp. Pass trail on right to Grace Lake. Reach Lake Solitude (9274). Camp here. 11 miles.

Second Day. Return to Paint Rock Lakes and parked car.

Observation This is very easy going. A lot of open hiking with little change in elevation.

Trip B 34½ miles, loop hike: 4 days, 3 nights
Start as in Trip A to Teepee Pole Flats. Here take F.S. Trail 38 left up North Paintrock Creek. Reach junction of F.S.

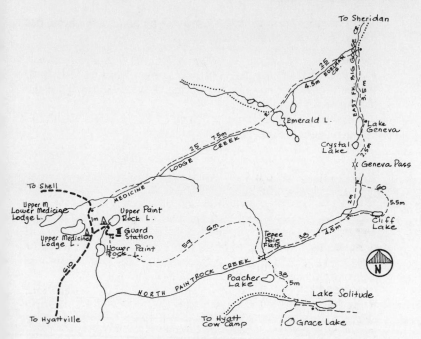

Trail Map for Trips A and B

Trail 60 on right to Cliff Lake. Take the trail to camp at lake. 11 miles.

Second Day. Continue on F.S. Trail 60 and climb to Geneva Pass (10300). Descend steeply to pass Crystal Lake (9700) and reach Lake Geneva (9283). Camp here. 7 miles.

Third Day. Descend along East Fork of Big Goose Creek. Reach junction of F.S. Trail 25 on left leading to Emerald Lake. Ascend this trail along Edelman Creek. Cross Edelman Pass (10360). Reach Emerald Lake (10250). Camp here. 8 miles.

Fourth Day. Ascend from Emerald Lake to pass at 10,465 feet and start descent along Medicine Lodge Creek to Paint Rock Lakes. Reach F.S. Road 610 and hike last mile on road to parked car and campgrounds. 8½ miles.

Observation Another comfortable route. Fine open-country hiking at alpine altitudes.

MONTANA

This state is the fourth largest in the country with 147,000 square miles of towering mountains and spreading prairies. It is a land of remote wilderness, forgotten towns, and a rich frontier history of exploration, trapping, and gold.

The eastern part of the state is prairie, while in the western forest lands the high peaks and rugged slopes make up the Continental Divide. All of western Montana is hiking country. There are popular routes, and others leading to remote areas seldom traveled. This chapter describes several of the latter.

In this western third of the state are the extensive national forests with their lakes and streams, tall trees, and abundant wildlife. Several forest and mountain areas have been set aside to remain as wilderness or primitive lands.

Montana is a state of trails. Through the forests and over the mountains Indians, trappers, and explorers made their early routes: the old West Trail, the Bannock Trail, and the Lewis and Clark Trail, which cover almost 2,000 miles of Montana. Then came the loggers and miners. Since those times many more trails have been made by forest management for access and recreation.

Montana has many splendid hiking areas. A backpacker can remain for weeks in the Bob Marshall Wilderness or spend a few days in Spanish Peaks Primitive Area. The grandeur of Glacier National Park beckons every hiker.

GLACIER NATIONAL PARK

This is a large park, comprising 1,013,000 acres. It contains 900 miles of trails in spectacular mountain country bordering Canada in the Rocky Mountains. The fishing is good, and the wildlife includes elk, moose, mountain goats, bighorn sheep, and bears.

To obtain map-brochures, write Glacier National Park, West Glacier, Montana 59936.

ANACONDA-PINTLAR WILDERNESS

This 157,803-acre wilderness area is in southwestern Montana, a rugged land of scenic, mountainous beauty astride the Continental Divide for 30 miles. As part of the Anaconda Range in the Rocky Mountains, this wilderness is a land of thin soils and snow-topped rocky mountains, glacier-formed valleys, sparkling streams, and many lakes fed by everlasting snowbanks. From the peaks along the Continental Divide hikers can look out over the Mission Mountains to the northwest and the Bitterroot Range to the southwest.

This Wilderness was named after Charles Pintlar, a pioneer trapper who settled here and explored the area. Another "tall" man in the area's history was Martin (Seven Dog) Johnson, a trapper of great strength and endurance who was said to have trapped mountain goats and packed them out to zoos.

Blight played a disastrous role in the surrounding forest's history. In 1930-31 a pine beetle infestation destroyed about half the lodgepole and whitebark pines. The dead trees are still in evidence throughout the area, at the foot of the new forest growing up the mountainsides.

This part of the Anaconda Range is mostly granitic intrusion; it consists of folded and faulted sedimentary rocks in the north of the Wilderness and granitic crystalline rocks in the south.

The area is a splash of color in summer. Delicate wild flowers blanket the forests and fields at high altitudes. Buttercups, shooting stars, and spring beauties show up in late July.

Chances of seeing game are excellent in the backcountry. Look for mountain goats along the ridges and on the flats atop the mountains. Also to be seen are elk, moose, deer, bear, and a variety of smaller animals. Clark's nutcracker, Steller's jay, ravens, eagles, hawks, and owls are all inhabitants of these mountains.

Season July through mid-September. After July 15 for some trails.

Location The Anaconda-Pintlar Wilderness is located in the southwestern corner of Montana along the Continental Divide and overlapping three national forests: Deerlodge, Bitterroot, and Beaverhead.

Access The Wilderness can be reached from several points on its boundary. State 43 passes its southern border, U.S. 93 is close to the west border, while U.S. 10A and State 38 pass along its east and north borders respectively. Interstate 90 (east-west) brings traffic to these roads.

Transportation Services Bus service to Anaconda.

Accommodations Hotels, motels, and resorts are to be found on all the roads mentioned above. Numerous campgrounds surround the area.

Medical Assistance Anaconda and Hamilton in Montana. Salmon in Idaho.

Fishing Cutthroat and rainbow trout in most lakes and streams. Eastern brook trout in some streams below 7,000 feet. Buy a license locally or write Montana Fish and Game Commission, Mitchell Building, Helena, Montana 59601.

Hunting This area is open to hunting during regular seasons. Deer, elk, and bear are the regular game, while drawings are made for license to take sheep, goats, antelope, and moose. For more information write the same address above.

Recreation Off the trails, Montana hikers can visit many places of interest. Boom days live again in the restored towns of Nevada City and Virginia City. This is Alder Gulch territory, where rich gold placer diggings were discovered in 1863. Take State 287 south of Butte.

In Anaconda is the world's largest smokestack at the Anaconda Smelter. A few miles east is Butte, where they still dig in the open pits of the world's "richest hill." Museum of mining is located here.

West of the Wilderness, on U.S. 93, see the Bitterroot Valley with St. Mary's Mission, established in 1841, and Fort Owen.

Wilderness Trails Many miles of trails provide access to the wonders of this Wilderness. A 45-mile trail along the Continental Divide takes you past alpine lakes, across streams, under the shadow of snowcapped peaks, and over passes where a hiker has the chance to view wild game. This route forms the backbone of the trail system here.

There are a variety of trails, hard and easy. On any one hike you will encounter both. Trail heads are marked, as are junctions. Trails are not paint-blazed (there are old cut blazes on some trees) but easily followed. If in doubt, look for a trail in the path made where the Forest Service cut downed trees to make access for horse travel.

The water in the high country is unpolluted and safe to drink.

No fire permit is required. Camp can be made anywhere, preferably where others have already camped.

It would be easy to stay in this wilderness for weeks.

References Write for map-brochure, *Anaconda-Pintlar Wilderness,* address as above.

7½-minute quadrangles: Lower Seymour Lake, Pintlar Lake, Warren Peak, Long Peak.

Note: These topographic maps will be only of partial help. Much of this area has yet to be mapped.

Trip Outlines

Trip A   33 miles, loop hike: 4 days, 3 nights
Base at Lower Seymour Campground (6700), 11 miles west of Wise River, 4 miles north on County 274, and 6 miles northwest on F.S. Road 934. Trail leaves the north end of campground by well pump. Hike upstream to Upper Seymour Lake to camp first night. 8 miles.

Second Day. Climb to pass on Continental Divide and down to junction F.S. Trail 9. Go left to pass Page and Flower lakes and into Queener Basin. Kurt Peak, Queener Mountain (10074) and Fish Peak (10240) on your left. Camp below Cutaway Pass. 8 miles.

Third Day. Climb to Cutaway Pass (9400) and descend via switchback to junction of F.S. Trail 126. Turn left here to follow West Fork LaMarche Creek downstream to junction of F.S. Trail 132. Camp here or anywhere along the creek. 10 miles.

Fourth Day. Take F.S. Trail 132 back to Lower Seymour Campground. 7 miles.

Observations   Mountain goats frequent the pass above

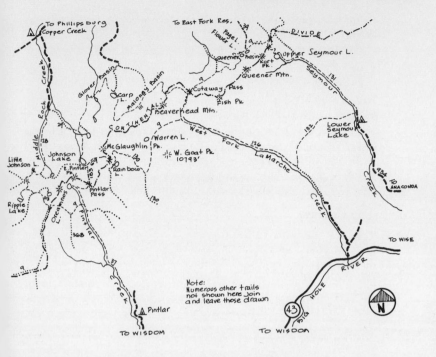

Trail Map for Trips A, B, C, D, and E

Upper Seymour Lake. On the second day there will be rugged hiking all day, but glorious vistas. Fishing is good here.

Trip B   20 miles, return hike: 3 days, 2 nights
Base at Pintlar Campground near the end of F.S. Road 185 north of Wisdom about 20 miles. Hike upstream on Pintlar Creek (F.S. Trail 37) to Oreamnos Lake (9365). Camp here. 8 miles.

Second Day. Leave camp at lake. Take a lunch and climb Pintlar Pass (8738) on F.S. Trail 183 to Johnson Lake. Descend to Johnson Lake. Or at Pintlar Pass hike the Continental Divide Ridge to East Pintlar Peak (9486). Return to Oreamnos Lake. 4 miles.

Third Day. Return downstream on F.S. Trail 37 to parked car. 8 miles.

Trip C   38 miles, one-way hike: 5 days, 4 nights
First and second day as in Trip A but on third day, after descending from Cutaway Pass, instead of turning left onto F.S. Trail 126 to descend West Fork LaMarche Creek, continue up F.S. Trail 9 to pass Warren Lake (8462) under West Goat Peak (10793) and descend to reach junction of F.S. Trail 130 leading right and up to Rainbow Lake (8215). Camp here. 9 miles.

Fourth Day. Climb Rainbow Pass (9040) on Continental Divide and descend to Johnson Lake (7720). Lunch here then take F.S. Trail 183 up to Pintlar Pass (8738) and descend; then ascend to camp at Oreamnos Lake (9365). 5 miles.

Fifth Day. Return downstream on F.S. Trail 37 to parked car above Pintlar Campground. 8 miles.

   Note: For information about trail conditions for the above hikes (A, B, C) write or visit District Ranger, Wise River Ranger Station, Wise River, Montana 59762.

Trip D   23 miles, loop hike: 3 days, 2 nights
Base at Copper Creek Campground (5900) about 6 miles south of Phillipsburg on U.S. 10A and 9 miles southwest on State 38, then south on F.S. Road 80. Park car at trail head beyond campground. Ascend F.S. Trail 28 along Middle Rock Creek to Little Johnson Lake and over Bitterroot Pass to Ripple Lake. Camp here. 7 miles.

Second Day. Retrace steps from Ripple Lake to take F.S. Trail 313 crossing Continental Divide and connecting with

F.S. Trail 9. Pass F.S. Trail 368, and join F.S. Trail 37 to Oreamnos Lake. Camp here. 8 miles.

Third Day. Climb Pintlar Pass (8738) on F.S. Trail 183 and descend to Johnson Lake (7720). Take F.S. Trail 29 down to parked car. 8 miles.

Trip E   51 miles, one-way hike: 6 days, 5 nights
As in Trip D until arriving at Johnson Lake on third day. Instead of returning to parked car at trail head, continue on to Glover Basin. Camp here. 9 miles.

Fourth Day. Continue to Carp Lake and junction of F.S. Trail 111. Take this trail over Warren Pass into Maloney Basin. Camp here. 8 miles.

Fifth Day. Cross Continental Divide again north of Beaverhead Mountain (9804) and follow just below ridge to cross divide again at Cutaway Pass (9400) and junction of F.S. Trail 9. Descend F.S. Trail 9 to F.S. Trail 38. Camp here. 9 miles.

Sixth Day. Continue on F.S. Trail 9 into Queener Basin. Pass Flower Lake and Page Lake. Reach junction with F.S. Trail 39. Take this trail downstream to parked car at south end of East Fork Reservoir. 10 miles.

Note: For information about trail conditions for the above hikes (D and E) contact District Ranger, Deerlodge Ranger Station, Phillipsburg, Montana 59858.

BIGHORN CANYON NATIONAL RECREATION AREA

This is a very dry area of 123,000 acres. It contains a reservoir 71 miles long, mostly in a steep-walled canyon. Although there are no trails, the fishing is good, and hunting is permitted. The forests at higher elevations shelter elk, deer, black bear, and wild horses. Fossil hunters will find the area rewarding.

Map-brochures are available from the following address: Bighorn Canyon Recreation Area, P.O. Box 458 Y.R.S., Hardin, Montana 59035

BEARTOOTH PRIMITIVE AREA

This 230,000-acre wild preserve is in the heart of one of the most wonderful high-mountain areas in America. The Beartooth High Lake Country is a land of many glacier-flanked peaks rising above 12,000 feet, vast plateaus above 11,000 feet, and hundreds of lakes and waterfalls. The Beartooth Highway, a winding route to the top of this country, will give visitors spectacular views of the high plateaus, glaciers, and peaks.

The exposed rocks of the Beartooths are the oldest known to us. Gneiss, mica schist, and quartzite were formed 2.7 billion years ago. Their shaping started some 75 million years ago under gradual compressing, folding, and uplifting. Topped by sandstone and limestone, the rock was uplifted several thousand feet. The elements have gradually worn away most of this soft capping. Great glaciers scraped out valleys, while rivers carried off the debris to leave the mountains as we see them today.

And in those glaciated valleys, with their meadows and numerous lakes, are moose, deer, and bear. Bighorn sheep and goats frequent the plateaus and summits.

Mountain slopes are green with pine, spruce, fir, and aspen. Alpine meadows support a variety of wild flowers. The pink snow seen on the perpetual snowbanks is actually microscopic plants growing on the surface.

Season July through mid-September. After July 15 for some trails. June and September are usually rainy months.

Expect severe storms and snow anytime during July and August at high altitudes.

Location   The Beartooth Primitive Area is located on the southern border of Montana, north of Yellowstone National Park, in the Custer and Gallatin national forests.

Access   U.S. 212 provides the only major road to the area. Interstate 90 (east-west) brings traffic to U.S. 212.

Transportation Services   Bus service to Red Lodge.

Accommodations   Hotels, motels, resorts along U.S. 212 between Red Lodge and Cooke City.

Medical Assistance   Red Lodge.

Fishing   Countless streams and lakes provide excellent fishing here. The catch can include whitefish, a rare grayling, or any one of the trouts. For an excellent guide to the where and what of Beartooth fishing write for a copy of *Index of Lakes, Beartooth High Lake Country* and its companion map, Supervisor, Custer National Forest, 2602 First Avenue North, Billings, Montana 59103.

Buy a license locally or for more information write Montana Fish and Game Commission, Mitchell Building, Helena, Montana 59601.

Hunting   The big game favorite is deer. Occasionally hunters take elk, bear, moose, bighorn sheep, and goat. For seasons and license information contact same address as above.

Recreation   Just a few miles from here is Yellowstone National Park with its hot geysers, bears, and wonderful scenery.

To the north is Livingston, the site of Captain Clark's arrival at the Yellowstone River as he headed back east in

1806. Trout derby here in August and an annual rodeo on July 4.

To the east of Beartooth Country is Billings with its Yellowstone Museum, Range Rider Monument, and Boothill Cemetery. Nearby is the Pictograph State Park Monument. Further east is Pompey's Pillar, a 200-foot rock formation and landmark where Captain Clark carved his name July 25, 1806.

Wilderness Trails This area provides a backpacker with a variety of trails that will take him into incredible scenic lake country and tundralike plateaus, to 12,000-foot peaks and down through grassy meadows. The trail system in the Primitive Area is not a large one, although the surrounding forests have a number of trails. The Primitive Area, with its vast plateaus, allows for challenging cross-country trips for the experienced hiker.

The trails numbered are easy to follow. Trail heads and junctions are signed.

Water is plentiful and safe in the high country.

No fire permit is required. Camp can be made anywhere, preferably where others have already been.

References Write for map-brochure, *Beartooth Primitive Area,* District Ranger, Rock Creek Ranger Station, Red Lodge, Montana 59068.

15-minute quadrangles: Mt. Maurice, Alpine, Cooke City, and Mt. Wood.

Trip Outlines

Trip A   18 miles, one way: 3 days, 2 nights
Just south of Red Lodge on U.S. 212 take F.S. Road 71 to parking at end of road (8000). Take F.S. Trail 1 up West Fork Rock Creek. Pass Calamity Falls. Pass Sentinel Falls. Reach Quinnebaugh Meadows. 3,000-foot cliffs of Silver Run Peak on left. Camp in meadow near treeline. 6 miles.

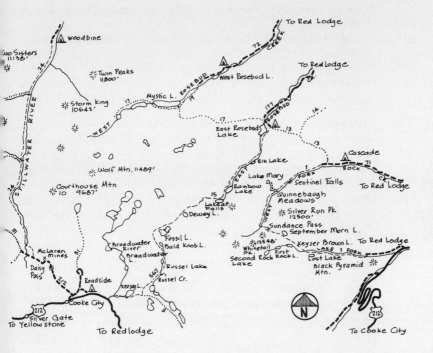

Trail Map for Trips A, B, and C

Second Day. Hike above treeline. Ascend and pass above Sundance Lake (9400). Start steep climb via switchbacks to Sundance Pass. Wonderful vistas. Reach Sundance Pass (11000) and descend to September Morn Lake (9696). Camp here. 5 miles.

Third Day. Enter treeline and descend to pass Keyser Brown Lake (8700) and Lost Lake (8500). Reach parking on spur road from U.S. 212 and north of Black Pyramid Mountain. 7 miles.

Observation This is a delightful hike. Both the first and third days are easy going. The second day leads to incredible scenery. You may decide to remain another day at September Morn Lake. This is fishing country. A day hike to Keyser Brown Lake or First Rock and Second Rock lakes will surely produce a trout dinner.

Trip B   24 miles, one way: 3 days, 2 nights
Start hike about 3 miles east of Cooke City on U.S. 212 where Broadwater River, Broadwater Lake, and Kersey Lake trails meet U.S. 212 (8020). Hike to Kersey Lake (8070) on F.S. Trail 3. About a half-mile beyond the lake take F.S. Trail 567, climbing up Russel Creek to Russel Lake (8800). Continue ascending to leave treeline and reach Bald Knob Lake (9400) and the southern edge of a plateau with countless lakes. Camp here. 8 miles.

Second Day. Reach Fossil Lake (9900). Trail is now F.S. Trail 15. Descend to pass lakes and falls along East Rosebud Creek to Lake at Falls (8100). Camp here. 8 miles.

Third Day. Continue downstream. Pass Rainbow Lake (7600). Pass Elk Lake. Reach East Rosebud Lake (6200) and parked car on F.S. Road 177, 13 miles from Red Lodge via State 307 and county roads. 8 miles.

Trip C   24 miles, one way: 3 days, 2 nights
Southwest of the Primitive Area, just east of Cooke City (7651) on U.S. 212, take F.S. Road 212 northwest over Daisy Pass (9712) and down past old McLaren Mines to where F.S. Trail 24 meets road (8900). Take trail and descend alongside Stillwater River to parked car at Woodbine Campground (5300) on northernmost border of Primitive Area.

About 24 miles, descending over 3,600 feet. A very easy hike while surrounded by towering peaks.

FLINT CREEK RANGE

East of Phillipsburg there is a range of mountains running north and south for about 25 miles. This area of 9,000-foot peaks and countless lakes is seldom used by hikers. Many trails and abandoned roads crisscross the forests. Access to it can be from Phillipsburg or any of the campgrounds surrounding it.

SAPPHIRE MOUNTAINS

West of Phillipsburg there is a large area of Deerlodge National Forest that can provide excellent wilderness backpacking. Many of these mountains almost reach 9,000 feet. While there are fewer lakes here than in the Flint Creek Range, there are also fewer access roads. Numerous trails can take a hiker into wilderness for many days.

References For both Flint Creek Range and Sapphire Mountains, write for map-brochure showing Phillipsburg Ranger District in Deerlodge National Forest to District Forest Ranger, Phillipsburg Ranger Station, Phillipsburg, Montana 59858. Or when in the area, visit the station for firsthand information and suggested trips.

30-minute quadrangles: Sapphire. There are no topo maps of Flint Creek Range.

IDAHO

Idaho is truly the wilderness state. Almost the entire northern two-thirds of the state is comprised of national forest lands. Vast areas remain roadless, and many sections of the national forests qualify for wilderness status. Generally the southern part of the state is dry and hilly, while the northern part is mountainous. The Continental Divide follows a good portion of Idaho's eastern border with Montana.

Here is big game hunting at its best. Fishermen take native trout from high-country lakes, and hikers can trek into complete wilderness. Several regions have been set aside to remain wilderness and primitive. Through these areas, as well as the multiple-use forests, are many hundreds of miles of trails.

SAWTOOTH PRIMITIVE AREA

These 200,942 acres of wilderness straddle the spectacular peaks of the Sawtooth Range, 42 of which reach 10,000 feet or more. It would be difficult to find a more scenic land in America. Jagged toothlike mountains tower above plunging gorges, snowbanked glacial basins, alpine lakes, and soft green meadows frequented by deer and elk and a variety of smaller animals and birds.

The Sawtooth Primitive Area lies mostly in the Boise and Sawtooth national forests. The northern tip reaches into Challis National Forest. The prominent feature, the Sawtooth Range, is part of the Idaho Batholith, a great thrusting up of granitic rock, extensively glaciated to give the mountains their form.

Mountain goats, bighorn sheep, and cougar reside in this high country. Chinook and sockeye salmon spawn in the headwaters of the nearby Salmon River.

Timbered slopes and valleys include species of pine, fir, and spruce. Wild flowers blanket the alpine meadows and trail sides.

Season July through mid-September. After July 15 for some trails.

Location The Sawtooth Primitive Area is located in central Idaho.

Access   U.S. 93 passes the east border of the area, while State 21 curves around the north and west borders. These are the only main roads that provide access to the area. Numerous dirt roads lead to trail heads. Interstate 80 (east-west) brings traffic to U.S. 93.

Transportation Services   None.

Accommodations   Motels in Stanley. A lodge at Redfish Lake. Sun Valley is about 50 miles south.

Medical Assistance   Sun Valley.

Fishing   Trout in the lakes and streams. Buy a license locally or write Idaho Department of Fish and Game, 500 Front Street, Boise, Idaho 83702.

Hunting   Big game here include deer, elk, mountain goat, and bear. For seasons, limit and license information write as above.

Recreation   Nearby Sun Valley provides all that is expected for a fine vacation. This picturesque village has year-around ice skating along with horseback riding, tennis, golf, and a variety of other sports and pastimes.

On U.S. 93 east of the Sawtooth is Idaho's Petrified Forest. A little further east on Alt. U.S. 93 is the Miniature Grand Canyon on a fork of the Salmon River.

Craters of the Moon National Monument is south 125 miles on Alt. U.S. 93. Cinder cones, lava flows, and strange formations in a desolate region.

Wilderness Trails   The Sawtooth Primitive Area provides hikers with outstanding trails, vistas, and fishing. Many trails are in the shadow of craggy peaks and dense forests. Streamside routes lead to countless lakes where the chances of seeing game are excellent.

The trails are in good condition and easy to follow. Trail

heads are generally marked or easy to find. Junctions are signed also.

Water is abundant and unpolluted.

Fire permits are not required. Campsites can be made anywhere, preferably where others have already been.

References Write for map-brochure of the Sawtooth Primitive Area, District Ranger, Stanley Ranger Station, Stanley, Idaho 50671. Also ask for map-brochure of Boise, Sawtooth, and Challis national forests.

7½-minute quadrangles: Snowyside Peak, Mt. Cramer, Stanley.

30-minute quadrangles: Bear Valley, Rocky Bar.

Trip Outlines

Trip A   33 miles, one way: 4 days, 3 nights
Start trail near Redfish Lake Lodge at chain barrier beside laundromat on the lodge's trailer parking road. Do not park here. Take road a few hundred yards to Bench Lakes Trail 101. Take this trail and hike a ridge overlooking Redfish Lake. Hike along Redfish Creek to Flatrock Junction. Camp here. 8 miles.

Second Day. Climb to Alpine Lake; then ascend steeply to cross Alpine-Baron Divide to Upper Baron Lake. This makes about a half-mile gain in elevation from Redfish Lake. A good lunch stop here after about 4 miles. Outstanding views east and west. Continue on to descend to Baron Lake. Reach Baron Creek and descend along stream. Baron Peak on right (10307). Reach Moolack Creek. Camp here. 10 miles, mostly descending.

Third Day. Reach junction of North Fork Baron Creek and ascend trail around Mount Regan to Sawtooth Lake. Camp here. 9 miles.

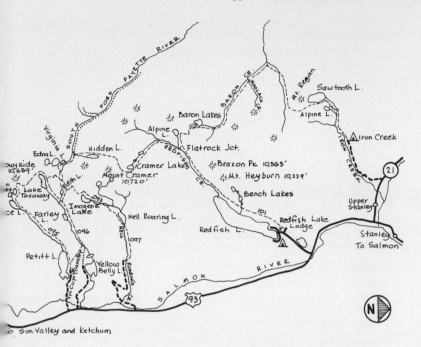

Trail Map for Trips A, B, C, and D

Fourth Day. Continue to Alpine Lake and descend to Iron Creek Campground and parking. 6 miles. The campground is 4 miles south of State 21 and west of Stanley.

Trip B 29 miles, one way: 4 days, 3 nights
Start trail as above in Trip A. Camp at Flatrock Junction, 8 miles.

Second Day. Move up to Upper Cramer Lake, cross ridge, and descend to Hidden Lake. Camp here. 8 miles.

Third Day. Reach junction of South Fork Payette River.

Climb to Virginia Lake, Edna Lake, and Sand Mountain Pass. Descend to Lake Toxaway and camp here. 6 miles.

Fourth Day. Continue up, cross ridge and descend to Twin Lakes and Alice Lake. Descend on F.S. Trail 095 to parking at transfer station on north side of Pettit Lake. About 11 miles, mostly descending.

Observations Excellent trail with two divides to cross and an ascent of nearly 3,000 feet. Matchless views of the country from these divides: Snowyside Peak, Mt. Cramer, Mt. Heyburn. Good fishing here, too.

Trip C 22½ miles, one way: 4 days, 3 nights
Start trail at Tin Cup Transfer on north side of Pettit Lake. Ascend to Alice Lake and Twin Lakes on F.S. Trail 095. Camp here below Snowyside Peak. 7 miles.

Second Day. Climb up and over ridge to Lake Toxaway. Camp here. 4 miles.

Third Day. Descend to junction of trail to Edith Lake. Ascend to Edith Lake and continue over divide to Imogene Lake. Camp here. 5½ miles.

Fourth Day. Descend along F.S. Trail 092 to Hell Roaring Lake, and hike down along Hell Roaring Creek on F.S. Trail 097 to Hell Roaring Road head and parking. Almost 6 miles.

Observations This makes an excellent fishing trip with short mileage days. Good trails to hike with about 2,400-foot rise. Spectacular scenery all the way.

Trip D 18 miles, loop hike: 3 days, 2 nights
Start as in Trip C; first and second days the same.

Third Day. Descend to pass junction of trail to Edith Lake. Keep on F.S. Trail 096 to pass Farley Lake and take Pettit Lake Cutoff Trail before reaching Yellow Belly Lake. Reach parking at Tin Cup Transfer Camp. 7 miles.

CHAPTER 5

TRAILS FAR WEST

THE PACIFIC COASTAL states have in their Cascade and Sierra ranges examples of the most beautiful scenery in America. The Cascades, although generally not as high as the wild Sierras, display the same winter snows lingering into midsummer to water alpine meadows and fill trout streams. Here are the eastern peaks of the Pacific Ring on Fire, a series of volcanoes rimming the Pacific Ocean. Few sights are more exciting than viewing the singular peaks, Mts. Rainier, Shasta, and Hood.

The Sierras boast Mt. Whitney and spectacular high country abundant with water, flora, and fauna. Consistent good weather and a lack of rain makes backpacking comfortable. Small wonder California is a hiking state.

And other places draw outdoorsmen to the Far West. For those who want it, there are deserts and canyons, drier and warmer regions of generally lower elevation, yet excellent backcountry. The Coastal Range in California is the choice of many, especially for those who want to stay away from heavily used areas. Washington's Olympic National Park, with almost a million acres of mountainous rain forest, is in a category of its own. Certainly a hiker will find it difficult to beat this region of glacier-topped mountains and forests.

PACIFIC CREST TRAIL

Traveling the backbone of the Cascades and Sierras is the longest trail in America, the Pacific Crest National Scenic Trail, 2,350 miles long. This is a summit trail taking a hiker to incredibly beautiful forest, mountain, and alpine scenery. The route is complete in Washington and Oregon. Very small segments remain unfinished in California, although cross-country hiking will allow anyone to complete the trip. Allow 5 months for this greatest of all hiking adventures. Write for very complete map-brochures. For Washington or Oregon: Regional Forester, P.O. Box 3623, Portland, Oregon 97208. For California: Regional Forester, 630 Sansome Street, San Francisco, California 94111.

WILDERNESS AND PRIMITIVE AREAS

For information on wilderness and primitive areas in the Pacific coastal states, write the regional headquarters of the USDA Forest Service given below. Each wilderness or primitive area is listed under the address of the regional headquarters which has jurisdiction over it. (P) stands for primitive area, (W) for wilderness area.

CALIFORNIA REGION
630 Sansome Street
San Francisco, California 94111

Agua Tibia (P)
Caribou (W)

Glacier Peak in Eagle Cap Wilderness, Oregon—
U.S. Forest Service photo

Cucamonga (W)
Desolation (W)
Dome Land (W)
Emigrant Basin (P)
High Sierra (P)
Hoover (W)
John Muir (W)
Marble Mountain (W)
Minarets (W)
Mokelumne (W)
Salmon Trinity Alps (P)
San Gabriel (W)

San Gorgonio (W)
San Jacinto (W)
San Rafael (W)
South Warner (W)
Thousand Lakes (W)
Ventana (W)
Yolla Bolly-Middle Eel (W)

PACIFIC NORTHWEST REGION
P.O. Box 3623
319 SW Pine Street
Portland, Oregon 97208

Diamond Peak (W)
Eagle Cap (W)
Gearhart Mountain (W)
Glacier Peak (W)
Goat Rocks (W)
Kalmiopsis (W)
Mount Adams (W)
Mount Hood (W)
Mount Jefferson (W)
Mount Washington (W)
Mountain Lakes (W)
Pasayten (W)
Strawberry Mountain (W)
Three Sisters (W)

CALIFORNIA

Whereas Idaho might be called the *wilderness* state,
California could certainly be named the *trail* state. Or *hiking*
state. This state has a history of involvement with developing

outdoor recreation. In 1864 California initiated the state park concept when Congress transferred Yosemite Valley and the Mariposa Grove of Sierra redwoods to the state. California later gave it back to the National Park System. Now there are 200 parts to California's park system, comprising over 800,000 acres of parks, campgrounds, beaches, and places of historical interest.

More people hike here than anywhere else. The nation's largest hiking-conservation organization, the Sierra Club, was founded here. (Incidentally, the Sierra Club publishes a number of trail guidebooks and reference titles that will be of interest to most hikers. Some of these books are beautiful editions concerned with environmental issues and our nation's natural wonders. For a list of books write the Sierra Club, 1050 Mills Tower, San Francisco, California 94104.)

There is a fine system of national parks and forests in California, vast areas in the northern, southwestern, and eastern regions where timbered mountains, lakes and streams, deserts and canyons provide countless outdoor experiences for those willing to make the effort to enter these wildernesses. For many millions these recreation lands are only a few hours' drive from their homes.

The Cascade Range and the Sierra Nevadas stretch north-south on most of California's eastern border. A long hot valley is located in the central and southeastern part of the state, while another range of mountains extends the length of the state on its Pacific border. Most of the trails have been developed in these mountainous regions. The Pacific Crest Trail is the major link in these trail systems.

DESOLATION WILDERNESS

This 63,469 acres of mountain-lake country is a popular and beautiful retreat for the backpacker. Most of the area is above 6,500 feet with some peaks almost reaching 10,000 feet. Great ice flows moved over this area long ago, scraping away at all but the highest mountains and leaving more than 80 lakes. An average of 30 feet of snow falls on this area every winter, though it sees little rain. The snowmelt fills the lakes and streams, and greens the alpine slopes where mountain hemlock and heather grow. Struggling on the drier ridges and rocky summits sierra juniper survives the wintry blasts and lives where few trees could make it. This area is considered by many to be the finest hiking in the Sierra Nevada.

Season June through September. After July 15 to be sure high-country trails are open.

Location Desolation Wilderness is located just west of Lake Tahoe in the Sierra Nevada Mountains.

Access There are many points to enter the Wilderness. Trail heads are located around the borders and at the end of secondary roads reached by major highways. U.S. 50 brings traffic to the area from the west and east. State 89 passes along the area's east border.

Transportation Services Bus lines on U.S. 50 and State 89. Airlines to South Lake Tahoe.

Accommodations Motels and resorts throughout the area. Campgrounds in Eldorado National Forest as well as state and private campgrounds.

Medical Assistance South Lake Tahoe.

Fishing Trout stocked in the lakes. California license needed. Buy it locally or write Department of Fish and Game, Resources Building, 1416 Ninth Street, Sacramento, California 95814.

Hunting For game, seasons, and licenses write as above.

Recreation Lake Tahoe is a vacation center. There is everything here for those who want to go first class. The only competition near here is Reno, Nevada with its plush casinos and accommodations.

Southwest of the area and headed for Sacramento, stop at Placerville on U.S. 50. This town was formerly known as Hangtown, reflecting the summary justice of the region during the gold rush days.

Wilderness Trails There are over 75 miles of trails in this high-country area. The Pacific Crest Trail (north-south) is the main link in a system of trails begun when the Indians first ventured into this area from lower elevations. Later came trappers and explorers like Frémont and Carson. The gold rush brought other men and commerce. However, most of the trails remained at lower elevations surrounding the area. It was with the arrival of cattlemen and dairy farmers that some of the present-day routes in the high country were laid out. The Forest Service finished the job by constructing new trails linking together the earlier routes of Indians and pioneers.

Most of the trails are in good condition and signed.

Water is plentiful.

Permits are required. Write or visit District Ranger, Lake Valley Ranger Station, South Lake Tahoe, California 95705.

Camping is permitted anywhere, but try to use already established fireplaces.

This area is very well suited to day trips and overnighters. Access routes bring the hiker by car to the very boundary of the area in many cases. However, because this is a popular place, try to plan trips in midweek.

References Write for map-brochure, *Desolation Wilderness,* District Ranger, Lake Valley Ranger Station, South Lake Tahoe, California 95705.

7½-minute quadrangles: Rockbound Valley, Emerald Bay, Pyramid Peak, Echo Lake.

15-minute quadrangle: Fallen Leaf Lake.

A superb guidebook, *Desolation Wilderness* by Robert S. Wood, is available from Wilderness Press, Berkeley, California. $3.95. Check the book lists in backpacking gear catalogs.

Trip Outlines

Trip A   20½ miles, loop hike: 2½ days, 2 nights

From State 89, where it passes around the western end of Emerald Bay on Lake Tahoe, take the entrance road to Eagle Falls Campground. At the west end of the parking lot (6600) take F.S. Trail 17E03 leading to the Wilderness. Ascend from the canyon and cross bridge above Eagle Falls. Climb steeply through pine forest. Other trails split off; yet all come back as the trees are left and an open trail reaches the Eagle Lake Trail on right. Continue south and ascending, overlooking Eagle Lake. Reach a small meadow, a saddle, and then an easy descent before another climb through open timber to pass F.S. Trail 17E04 coming in on left from Emerald Bay. Pass unmarked trail on left to Azure Lakes and reach junction (8180) with trail to Dick's Pass. Turn to right and continue on F.S. Trail 17E34.1 through rolling woodlands, skirting numerous ponds, lakes, and campsites. Reach unmarked trail to Lower Velma Lake and then junction with F.S. Trail 17E34.2 leading west from the lakes to Camper Flat and Rockbound Valley. Reach Camper Flat and Pacific Crest Trail. Turn north to reach junction of F.S. Trail 16E04 to 4-Q Lakes (7500). Camp here. 7½ miles.

Second Day. Ford the arm of the largest lake or detour about 500 yards around the end of it. Skirt the lake and descend steeply along the stream emptying 4-Q Basin. In a wooded valley pass McConnell Lake outlet stream. Look for rock

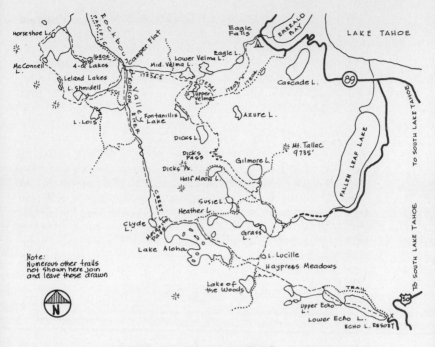

Trail Map for Trips A, B, and C

ducks (groups of two or three rocks stacked to mark trail) before reaching junction of Horseshoe Lake and 4-Q Lakes outlet creeks. The trail will cross both streams above rather than below their junctions as shown on maps. The trail moves up through forest and then onto granite slopes. Watch for rock ducks and faded red blazes. Reach Horseshoe Lake (7540) and meadow. Ascend along inlet stream to cross stream and hike under McConnell Peak. Reach McConnell Lake (7820) in a beautiful, peaceful meadow. Continue ascent to Leland Lakes along Leland Creek. Reach Leland

Lake (8160) and continue up out of Leland Lake Basin. Cross saddle and descend to Lake Schmidell to pass trail leading to Lake Lois. Continue on to Camper Flat and take trail to Velma Lakes Basin. Camp here. 8½ miles.

Third Day. Return to Eagle Falls Campground and parking. 4½ miles.

Trip B   6 miles, return trip: day hike
Leave U.S. 50 a mile west of Echo Summit and take winding paved road to parking, then on down to lake shore and Echo Lake Resort. Take boat-taxi through both Lower and Upper Echo lakes to the landing (7500). From landing join Pacific Crest Trail and ascend to Haypress Meadows (8300) and take trail to Lake of the Woods (8060). Lunch here. Return to public landing and take boat to end of Lower Echo Lake. About 6 miles, return trip.

Trip C   28½ miles, loop hike: 4 days, 3 nights
Starting as in Trip B. Instead of going to Lake of the Woods, continue on Pacific Crest Trail to Lake Aloha (8160). Cross Mosquito Pass (8420) and descend to reach trail leading down to Clyde Lake. This is where the Rubicon River starts down Rockbound Valley. Camp here. 6½ miles.

Second Day. Ascend from lake and continue north on Pacific Crest Trail down along the Rubicon River to Camper Flat. Leave Pacific Crest Trail and turn right to Middle Velma Lakes (7950). Reach junction with trail leading south to Fontanillis Lake (8300). Camp here. 8½ miles.

Third Day. Ascend to Fontanillis Lake, Dick's Lake, and Dick's Pass (9380). Descend to pass south of Gilmore Lake. Pass trails to Mt. Tallac and trail to Susie Lake. Pass trail from Glen Alpine Spring and Lily Lake. Reach trail to Grass Lake (7200). Camp here. 9 miles.

Fourth Day. Ascend to Lake Lucille (8200) and Lake Margery (8200). Reach Pacific Crest Trail and return to public landing at Upper Echo Lake via the Pacific Crest Trail. 4½ miles.

YOSEMITE NATIONAL PARK

Although this popular 761,000-acre park is overused and abused at present, it offers unsurpassed beauty in the Sierra Mountains. Scenic features include giant sequoias, waterfalls, and soaring peaks. The park boasts 749 miles of trails, including a portion of the Pacific Crest Trail.

Map-brochures are available from P.O. Box 577, Yosemite National Park, California 95389.

SALMON TRINITY ALPS PRIMITIVE AREA

At present writing this 225,000-acre area is under consideration for wilderness classification. It is rugged, wild country astride the Coast Range, with gray peaks reaching to 9,000 feet, ever present snowfields, rushing streams, and mirroring lakes. Scattered timber is found at higher elevations, while heavy growth covers the lower slopes and valleys.

Hudson Bay trappers were here after 1800. Then came trapper-explorers like Jedediah Smith. In the 1850's gold brought thousands into the canyons and mountains. Ghostly reminders of these efforts still remain throughout the area.

Once the grizzly bear and Roosevelt elk made a home here. Now deer, black bear, and occasional mountain lions are seen. And there was a time when silver salmon and steelhead trout crowded the streams. In fewer numbers they still spawn in the lower reaches of the big streams running from this primitive area.

Season Mid-June through September. August can be very

hot at lower elevations as one approaches the area. Above 3,000 feet it begins to cool.

Location The Salmon Trinity Alps Primitive Area is located in northwestern California, northwest of Redding.

Access The area is best reached from State 299 (east-west from Redding to Eureka) passing its southern border. Interstate 5 (north-south) brings traffic to Redding.

Transportation Services Bus service on State 299.

Accommodations Motels, resorts along State 299. Campgrounds in the surrounding national forests.

Medical Assistance Weaverville, east on State 299.

Fishing Trout in the stocked lakes and streams. Buy a license locally or write Department of Fish and Game, Resources Building, 1416 Ninth Street, Sacramento, California 95814. Ask for *Anglers Guide to the Lakes and Streams of the Trinity Alps*.

Hunting For game, season, licenses, write as above.

Wilderness Trails About 400 miles of trails await the hiker and backpacker here. Some of them follow old trails to gold mines and trappers' camps. Others are ridge trails that at once provide vistas toward the Pacific Ocean and the eastern Sacramento Valley. Many of the trails follow drainages in the shadow of rocky peaks and dense forests of pine and fir. Generally the eastern portion is alpine in appearance while the western part is lower in elevation.

The trails are in good condition and signed.

There is plenty of water once off the ridges.

A permit is rquired to enter the area. Write or visit District Ranger, Big Bar Ranger Station, Big Bar, California 96010.

References Write for *Forest Visitor's Map,* Trinity Na-

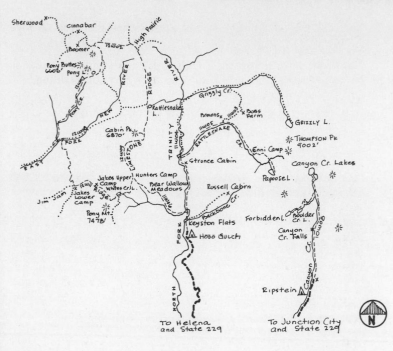

Trail Map for Trips A, B, and C

tional Forest, Humboldt and Mt. Diablo Meridians, District
Ranger, Big Bar Ranger Station, Big Bar, California 96010.

15-minute quadrangles: Helena, Ironside Mountain, Salmon Mountain, Cecilville.

Trip Outlines

Trip A 49 miles, loop hike: 6 days, 5 nights
From State 299 just west of Helena take the 16-mile road to
Hobo Gulch Campground (3000) at the edge of the Primitive

Area. This is a rough narrow road, but passable with patience. Following North Fork Trinity River, hike to Keystone Flats. Pass Backbone Creek and trail leading to Russell Cabin on right. Reach trail leading to Bear Wallow Meadows on left. Take this trail (F.S. Trail 11W06) to cross White's Creek and ascend through Bear Wallow Meadows, pass campsites, and continue on to reach Hunters Camp. Camp here. 7 miles.

Second Day. Ascend to ridge and F.S. Trail 12W09. Turn north along ridge. Fine vistas here looking east to high peaks of Primitive Area. Reach trail leading to Cabin Peak and Lookout (6870). Ascend this trail one mile for lunch stop. After lunch descend to ridge trail and continue north to campsite at Rattlesnake Lake. Camp here. 9 miles.

Third Day. Continue along ridge trail to reach junction with F.S. Trail 12W02 leading across High Prairie to west. Reach F.S. Trail 12W07 leading left and south off ridge and down to lakes and meadow under eastern slopes of Pony Buttes (6606). Camp. 8 miles.

Northwest of here are many abandoned gold mines: the Boomer, Cinnabar, Sherwood, and others. Ghost towns and crumbling ruins are all that remains of the fleeting prosperity once found here.

Fourth Day. Ascend from meadow, pass Pony Lake, and drop into Pony Creek drainage along F.S. Trail 12W07. Reach junction with F.S. Trail 12W08 and East Fork New River. Camp here. 8 miles.

Fifth Day. Ascend F.S. Trail 12W08 about one-half mile east until reaching trail on right. Ascend this steeply to Jim Jam Ridge Trail 12W11, passing Jake's Lower Camp. This is the historied Jake's Hunting Ground area. During the 1880s Jake Hershberger hunted for the hard rock miners of the area, bringing into their camp deer, elk, and bear. Turn east on F.S. Trail 12W11 and reach Jake's Upper Camp (6500). Pass north of Pony Mountain (7478) and descend to White's Creek Lake (6000) and junction with F.S. Trail 12W09. Camp here. 8 miles.

Sixth Day. Take F.S. Trail 12W09 north to junction with F.S. Trail 11W06. Leave ridge here and descend to pass Hunters Camp; hike through Bear Wallow Meadows and down along White's Creek, returning to Hobo Gulch Campground. 9 miles.

Trip B   23 miles, return trip: 3 days, 2 nights
Start as above. Instead of taking trail left to Bear Wallow Meadows, continue on along banks of North Fork Trinity River. Pass Strunce Cabin (3150). Reach Rattlesnake Creek Trail on right (F.S. Trail 11W05), leading up Rattlesnake Creek. Take this to pass F.S. Trail 11W03 leading to Bob's Farm and Grizzly Creek. Continue on to reach Enni Camp (5500). Camp here. 9½ miles.

Second Day. Ascend to Bear Valley Meadows Camp (7000). From here take primitive trail (about one hour) down to Papoose Lake (6663) and excellent fishing. 2 miles.

Third Day. Return to Hobo Gulch Campground. 11½ miles. Or camp at junction of F.S. Trails 11W05 and 11W03 near abandoned Brown's Mine. 5 miles. On the fourth day return to the campground. 6½ miles.

Trip C   20 miles, return trip: 3 days, 2 nights
From State 299 at Junction City take 15-mile Canyon Creek Road to Ripstein Campground (2900) and end of road. Ascend F.S. Trail 10W08 leading to Canyon Creek Lakes and the alpine scenery of this area. Cross Bear Creek and pass McKay Camp. Make a lunch stop at Canyon Creek Falls (4500). Continue climbing to pass trail to Boulder Creek Lakes. Reach Canyon Creek Lakes. Camp here. 7½ miles.

Second Day. Return to trail leading right and up to Boulder Creek Lakes and then up to Forbidden Lake. Excellent fishing. Camp here. 4 miles.

Third Day. Return to Canyon Creek and descend to parked car at trail head. 8½ miles.

POINT REYES NATIONAL SEASHORE

This 65,000-acre peninsular park includes beaches, cliffs, grasslands, and forest. There is a lot of private land within the park's boundaries. For hikers, Point Reyes National Seashore offers 75 miles of trails and the chance to see whales, dolphins, sea otters, seals, and sea lions offshore. The saltwater fishing is good.

For map-brochures write Point Reyes National Seashore, Point Reyes, California 94956.

SEQUOIA AND KINGS CANYON NATIONAL PARKS

Over 800,000 acres of forested mountain country invite the hiker to this area on the western slopes of the Sierras. It is a land of the giant sequoia trees, numerous snow-capped peaks topping 11,000 feet, spectacular canyons, and breathless alpine scenery. It is a favorite jumpoff point to the High Sierras and the John Muir Wilderness.

Superlatives fit this land. It contains the world's largest living thing, a 3,000-year-old sequoia tree; Mt. Whitney (14495), the highest point in the contiguous 48 states; the Muir Trail (211 miles), the longest uninterrupted footpath in America; matchless weather, very little rain and balmy days with frosty mornings in the high country.

Season July through September. After July 15 for some of the high passes.

Location   The Sequoia and Kings Canyon national parks are located in mideastern California east of Fresno.

Access   The parks are best reached from the west side. State 180 and 198 bring traffic from State 99 running north-south from Fresno to Bakersfield.

Transportation Services   None.

Medical Assistance   Park first aid. Private assistance in Fresno or Visalia.

Fishing   In streams and lakes. Well stocked with brook, brown, golden, and rainbow. Buy a California license locally or write Department of Fish and Game, Resources Building, 1416 Ninth Street, Sacramento, California 95814.

Hunting   None.

Recreation   Within the parks are enough sites and points of interest to keep a vacationer here for several days. Ancient sequoia trees more than 3,000 years old, superb mountain scenery, waterfalls, and quiet meadows are all features of the parks.

Tours are conducted to caves, and nature walks are led by experienced naturalists. Evening campfire programs help visitors understand the parks.

A three-hour drive north will bring vacationers to the popular Yosemite Valley National Park.

San Francisco is another three-hour drive from the parks.

Park Trails   Many hundreds of miles of trails have been constructed in the parks and leading from the parks to the surrounding John Muir Wilderness. They start at lower elevations and reach toward the peaks. And within the parks there are many short trails that provide excellent day hike routes.

The trails are in good condition and signed.

Water is plentiful.

Permits are required. They can be had free from any of the Ranger Stations within the parks.

Campsites in the backcountry are numerous. Whenever possible camp at designated areas or established campsites.

References Write for map-brochure, *Sequoia and Kings Canyon National Parks,* Sequoia Natural History Association, Sequoia and Kings Canyon National Parks, Three Rivers, California 93271.

15-minute quadrangles: Marion Peak, Mt. Pinchot.

Trip Outlines

Trip A 43 miles, loop hike: 5 days, 4 nights

With a very early morning start take State 180 into Kings Canyon and beyond Cedar Grove Campground to Road's End and parking (5035). Permits can be had at Cedar Grove Ranger Station. Start the trip on an easy trail leading through ponderosa pines and up the north side of the South Fork of Kings River. Reach Bubbs Creek Bridge (5098) and fork in trail. Cross the bridge and start up Bubbs Creek, ascending easily. Good views here of the glaciated U-shaped canyon of South Fork Kings River. Also note the Sphinx, a prominent granite peak above the south wall of Bubbs Creek Canyon. Continue to ascend, passing single-leaf pinyon pines and reaching Sphinx Creek Trail junction on right (6250). Continue along Bubbs Creek to reach Charlotte Creek and forested glades of aspen, cottonwood, and bracken. Reach Junction Meadow (8160). Camp here at west end of meadow. 11½ miles.

Second Day. Leave meadow and ascend steeply through open manzanita-covered slopes to level off and reach Vidette Meadow (9600) and junction with John Muir Trail (211-mile segment of Pacific Crest Trail). Turning north here along Muir Trail, climb steeply out of Bubbs Creek Canyon. Wonderful

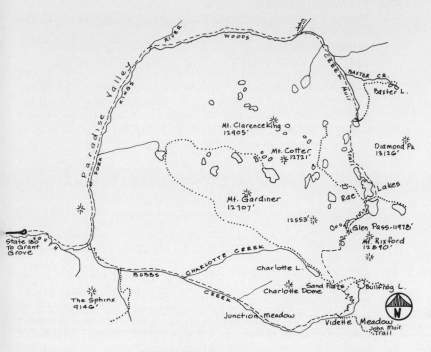

Trail Map for Trip A

views here of canyons and surrounding peaks. Reach Sand Flats (10700) and views of Sierra Crest Peaks. Continue on, passing trail down to Charlotte Lake (10320) and trail to Bullfrog Lake (10630). Pass above Charlotte Lake, its creek, and white granite Charlotte Dome. Above treeline now, hike to a small glacial pond in the cirque under Glen Pass. Camp here. 5½ miles.

Third Day. Ascend Glen Pass (11978) and its 3-foot-wide ridge trail. Magnificent views of peaks and lake country below.

Descend steeply via switchbacks to reach Rae Lakes area (10560). Explore this lakes area, making a camp in the vicinity. 5 miles.

Fourth Day. Leave lake area. Pass trail to Baxter Pass. Reach Woods Creek Crossing (8492) and the canyon terrain familiar from the first day's hiking. Leave John Muir Trail at this point and head down Woods Creek Canyon to Castle Domes Meadow (8300). Reach South Fork Kings River and Paradise Valley (6800). Camp here. 10 miles.

Fifth Day. Descend out of Paradise Valley. Reach Mist Falls (5663) and a good lunch stop. Reach level trail and Bubbs Creek Bridge (5098). Then on to parking at Road's End. 11 miles.

LASSEN VOLCANIC NATIONAL PARK

Lassen Peak, a plug-dome volcano 10,457 feet high, dominates the landscape of this 107,000-acre park. Scenic attractions of the alpine area include lava beds, hot springs, lakes, and mountains. White pelican, deer, fox, and black bear are found along the 150 miles of trails. Hikers should be prepared for cold weather in midsummer.

To obtain map-brochures, write Lassen Volcanic National Park, Mineral, California 96063.

OREGON

Oregon is a land of forests. Nearly half of the state's 62 million acres is forested. And half of this lies within 13 national forests. Eastern Oregon is generally flat with rolling hills. An exception to this are the mountainous regions in the northeast. Western Oregon is flanked by the Cascade Moun-

tains with their singular snowcapped peaks like Mt. Hood and
Mt. Jefferson, and the Coast Range along the Pacific Ocean. In
between is a fertile valley.

Wilderness areas are many, and the trails into them extensive. A backpacker can choose very remote country in the
northeast or hike into magnificent lake country along the Pacific Crest Trail in the Cascades.

EAGLE CAP WILDERNESS

This 220,416-acre Wilderness straddles the Wallowa Mountains. It is a land of rugged peaks, high slopes without timber,
glacial basins, and alpine lakes disgorging streams into lower
meadows. This is high country. Several peaks rise above 9,000
feet and many lakes dot the area. The exposed rock in the
mountains is predominantly granitic with some limestone, all
of which have undergone tremendous uplifting and warping
resulting in the present form that subsequently underwent ice
age glaciation. The elements have completed the picture of
today.

Season July through September. After July 15 for some
trails.

Location The Eagle Cap Wilderness is located in the
Wallowa-Whitman National Forest in northeastern Oregon.

Access Interstate 80 brings a hiker to the west side of the
area. State 203 services the west and south borders, while State
82 bends around the north border. The eastern border is inac-
cessible by other than dirt roads. Generally these roads are in
poor condition but passable.

Transportation Services None.

Accommodations Motels, resorts, and ranches throughout,
and in the below-mentioned towns.

Medical Assistance   Baker in the southwest. Enterprise and Wallowa in the north. Union in the west.

Fishing   Most lakes have eastern brook trout. Some have been stocked with golden, lake, and rainbow. Buy a license locally or write Oregon State Game Commission, 1634 S.W. Alder Street, Portland, Oregon 97205.

Hunting   Mountain goats near the Matterhorn and Hurwal-Hurricane Divide; deer, elk, and bear. For season, limits, and licenses write as above.

Wilderness Trails   This area is large enough, and the trails extensive enough, for the backpacker to stay out for weeks yet seldom retrace his steps.

Most of the trails are above 7,000 feet. All of the main peaks, Matterhorn (9845), Eagle Cap (9595), Sacajawea (9833), can be climbed without special equipment. The trails are easy to follow, signed at trailheads and junctions.

Water is plentiful.

Fire permits are not required. Camp can be made anywhere but try to use the designated areas at heavy use points.

References   Write for the map-brochure, *Eagle Cap Wilderness,* District Ranger, Baker Ranger Station, Baker, Oregon 97814. This is an excellent colored topo map with all the trails to the Wilderness. Also ask for the map-brochure of Wallowa-Whitman National Forest.

Trip Outlines

Trip A   19 miles, loop hike: 3 days, 2 nights
Start at end of Lostine River Road S202, about 18 miles south of Lostine on State 82. Two Pan Campground is here at 5,600 feet. Take F.S. Trail 1670 up Lostine River. Pass trail up Elkhorn Creek. Reach Minam Lake (7400). Camp here. 6 miles.

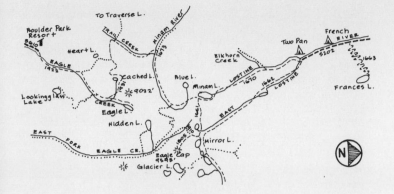

Trail Map for Trips A, B, and C

Second Day. Take F.S. Trail 1661 at south end of lake to ascend via switchbacks to ridge (8600). Above treeline here with grand views of surrounding peaks. Descend to Mirror Lake (7600). Lunch here and make camp. In the afternoon ascend Eagle Cap Mountain (9595) via F.S. Trails 1910 and 1805. Return to camp at Mirror Lake. 6½ miles.

Third Day. Return on F.S. Trail 1662 along East Lostine River to parking at end of S202. 6½ miles.

Observations Mirror Lake and the Lake Basin are always crowded. But to climb Eagle Cap Mountain, they provide the best camp spot.

Trip B 18 miles, return hike: 2 days, 1 night
Start where F.S. Trail 1663 meets Lostine River Road S202, about a mile north of French Campground. Steep ascent (3,200 ft.) by switchbacks on north side of Marble Point. Wonderful views on this hike; most of the trail is open to the surrounding

country. Top ridge at 8,600 feet and descend to Frances Lake (7800). Excellent fishing. 9 miles.

Second Day. Return to S202.

Trip C   25 miles, one way: 4 days, 3 nights
On the south side of the Wilderness start at Boulder Park Resort at end of S610 from Medicine Springs on State 203. Follow signs to Boulder Park Resort (5000). Take F.S. Trail 1922 and ascend Eagle Creek. Pass trail up Bench Creek to Heart Lake. Pass trail to Lookingglass Lake. Pass trail to Cached Lake. Reach Eagle Lake (7600). Camp here. 7 miles.

Second Day. Retrace steps to F.S. Trail 1931, leading to Cached Lake. Ascend to lake (7350). Climb to ridge above lake (8100). Descend to Trail Creek. Pass trail to Traverse Lake. Reach junction of F.S. Trail 1673 on Minam River (5360). Camp here. 7 miles.

Third Day. Descend Minam River on F.S. Trail 1673 to Minam Lake (7400). Camp here. 5 miles.

Fourth Day. Descend Lostine River Trail 1670 to end of Lostine River Road S202. 6 miles.
   Or on fourth day the hike can be routed as described in Trip A: Minam Lake to Mirror Lake, then up Eagle Cap and return to camp at Mirror Lake. Fifth day hike down East Lostine River Trail to Lostine River Road S202. This would make it 5 days and 32 miles.

CRATER LAKE NATIONAL PARK

The dominating feature of this 160,000-acre park is a beautiful blue lake in the heart of a dead volcano. Thirty-five miles of trails, including a portion of the Pacific Crest Trail, wind through coniferous forests and wild flowers.

Write to Crater Lake National Park, P.O. Box 7, Crater Lake, Oregon 97604 for map-brochures.

MT. JEFFERSON WILDERNESS

This 99,600 acres of mountains, lakes, and forests was recently made a wilderness area. Mt. Jefferson dominates the landscape. Its perpetual glaciers can be viewed from many miles away. Further south the pinacles of Three Fingered Jack rise above Marion Lake. One of these is frequently in sight while hiking.

Season July through September. After July 15 for high trails.

Location Mt. Jefferson Wilderness is located in the Deschutes, Mt. Hood, and Willamette national forests in north-central Oregon.

Access U.S. 20 and 126 pass the area's southern border, while State 22 provides access to the west border.

Transportation Services Bus service on U.S. 20 and 126 and State 22.

Accommodations Campgrounds surround the area.

Medical Assistance Marion Forks.

Fishing Trout in the streams and lakes stocked by the state. Buy a license locally or write Oregon State Game Commission, 1634 S.W. Alder Street, Portland, Oregon 97205.

Hunting For game, limits, seasons, and licenses write above address.

Recreation Not too many miles north from here is the recreation area of Mt. Hood, the highest point in Oregon at 11,245 feet. North of there is the Columbia River and

Portland. Three hours' drive west brings vacationers to the Pacific Ocean and places like Seal Rock and the great sand dunes of Umpqua Dunes Scenic Area.

Wilderness Trails There are over 200 miles of trails in this Wilderness. The Pacific Crest Trail (36.4 miles) forms the north-south link for the network of trails in this wilderness. There are many access points to enter the Wilderness, some more popular than others.

The trails are in good condition, signed at trail heads and junctions.

Water is plentiful.

Fire permits are not required. Camp can be made anywhere, but use designated areas when possible.

References Write for the excellent colored topo map, *Mt. Jefferson Wilderness,* District Ranger, Willamette National Forest, Detroit, Oregon 97342. Also ask for a copy of *Pacific Crest National Scenic Trail, Oregon.*

Trip Outlines

Trip A 28 miles, loop hike: 4 days, 3 nights
Begin where Santiam Lake Trail 3491 leaves U.S. 20 (4750) about a mile west of Santiam Pass. Hike north on very comfortable trail to Santiam Lake (5124). Three Fingered Jack on right. Pass F.S. Trail 3494 to Dixie Lakes and descend to Duffy Lake (4793). Camp here. 6 miles.

Second Day. On F.S. Trail 3422, move up to Mowich Lake and Alice Lake, round east side of Red Butte (5843), pass Red Butte Lake (5200), and descend gradually to pass many lakes before reaching Marion Lake (4130). Camp here. 7½ miles.

Third Day. Proceed on F.S. Trail 3437 on northeast side of lake and ascend gradually to junction with F.S. Trail 3492 to

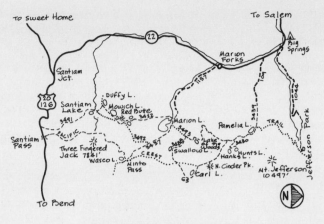

Trail Map for Trips A and B

Red Butte. Keep left and ascend more steeply to Minto Pass and junction with Pacific Crest Trail. Continue on over pass to Wasco Lake. Camp here. 5 miles.

Fourth Day. Retrace steps to Pacific Crest Trail and return south, passing west of Three Fingered Jack (7841) and descending to Santiam Pass Summit. Turn west on U.S. 20, and continue one mile to start of hike. 10½ miles. Note: no water on this section of trail.

Trip B   33 miles, loop hike: 5 days, 4 nights
On west side of Wilderness, about 2 miles north of Riverside Campground on State 22, take F.S. Road 109 east to end (3100). Start F.S. Trail 3439 here in the shadow of Mt. Jefferson. Ascend to Pamelia Lake (3884) and junction with Pacific Crest Trail. Continue on up steeply to junction with F.S. Trail 3430 (5000). Climb to Hunts Lake. Camp here. 6½ miles.

Second Day. Retrace steps down to Pacific Crest Trail and head south. Cathedral Rocks on left ahead. Pass west of North Cinder Peak (6722). About 1 mile beyond North Cinder Peak look for cutoff trail to Carl Lake. Descend to Carl Lake (5500). Camp here. 7 miles.

Third Day. Hike out of Carl Lake on F.S. Trail 65 and ascend to junction of Pacific Crest Trail and F.S. Trail 3488 leading down to pass lava beds and Swallow Lake. Continue on to junction with F.S. Trail 3493. Take this trail north to camp at Lake of the Woods (4800). 6½ miles.

Fourth Day. Continue on F.S. Trail 3493. Pass junction F.S. Trail 3421. Keep right. Ascend to junction of Pacific Crest Trail. Take this trail north to junction with F.S. Trail 3430 leading to Hunts Lake (campsite on first night). Take this trail again, but camp at Hanks Lake (5144). 7 miles.

Fifth Day. Return to Pacific Crest Trail and hike north and down to Pamelia Lake and junction with F.S. Trail 3439, returning to F.S. Road 109. 6 miles.

Other Trips Fine day hikes and overnight trips can be made here.

1. 5 miles ascending along F.S. Trail 3429 and Pacific Crest Trail to Jefferson Park. Start trail at end of F.S. Road 1044 leaving State 22, a half-mile east of Big Springs Campground.
2. 2½ miles along F.S. Trail 3436 to Marion Lake. Start trail at end of F.S. Road 1157 leaving State 22 just south of Marion Forks.

THREE SISTERS WILDERNESS

Almost 200,000 acres, this Wilderness straddles the Cascade Mountains for 29 miles in central Oregon. The Three Sisters, all of them over 10,000 feet, are found in the northern part of the Wilderness. In the south are countless lakes and connecting streams.

Lava beds in the north and central portion are a reminder of volcanic activity that once went on here. The Three Sisters are part of the series of volcanoes in the Cascade Mountains that began erupting 5 million years ago and continued to recent history. Glacial erosion has modified and reshaped these mountains, but there are several good examples of volcano cones.

Glaciers and lingering snowbanks perpetually cover portions of the peaks and high slopes. In the winter the snow is often 20 feet deep in some places. These great snowfields feed the streams, lakes, and green meadows gaily colored with an incredible variety of wild flowers: blue lupine, red Indian paintbrush, sunflowers, daisies, shooting stars, and others.

Douglas fir grows on the western slopes of the Cascades, ponderosa on the eastern slopes. Varieties of spruce, hemlock, and cedar are found at lower elevations. At higher elevations these trees are stunted, because of the limited growing season.

In the forests and on the trails a hiker has a good chance of seeing deer, elk, and black bear. The lucky hiker will spot a cougar. Raccoons, bobcats, coyotes, and muskrats are also in the area. Blue and ruffed grouse are found in the uplands.

Season July through September. After July 15 for some trails.

Location The Three Sisters Wilderness is located in central Oregon in the Willamette and Deschutes national forests.

Access State 242 passes the northern border of the Wilderness. State 58 and U.S. 126 provide major access to southern and western borders. U.S. 97 and State 46 are the routes to eastern borders.

Transportation Services Bus to Bend on U.S. 97.

Accommodations   Motels and resorts on all the above-mentioned roads. Campgrounds surround the area.

Medical Assistance   Bend on U.S. 97. Oakridge on State 58. Springfield on U.S. 126.

Fishing   There are over 300 lakes here, most of them with fish. They are annually stocked with rainbow, eastern brook, and cutthroat. Buy a license locally or write Oregon State Game Commission, 1634 S.W. Alder Street, Portland, Oregon 97205.

Hunting   Deer, elk, black bear, blue and ruffed grouse in the forest. For seasons, limits, licenses write same address as above.

Recreation   South of the Wilderness is the very beautiful Crater Lake National Park. This is a *must see* for all those who visit this area. Further south and east are the Oregon National Monument and Rogue River country in the Siskiyou National Forest.

Wilderness Trails   As is the case with most of the trails along the Cascade Mountains, the 240 miles of trails here lead to summits, streams, and meadows. The Pacific Crest Trail is the main route in a trail system that will allow a backpacker to spend many days in this wilderness.

The trails are in good condition, signed at all trail heads and junctions.

Water is plentiful.

Fire permits are not required. Camp can be made anywhere.

References   Write for map-brochure, *Three Sisters Wilderness,* District Ranger, Bend Ranger Station, 211 East Revere Street, Bend, Oregon 97701. This is a very detailed, colored topo map of the area with all its trails. Also ask for map-brochure of the Willamette and Deschutes national forests.

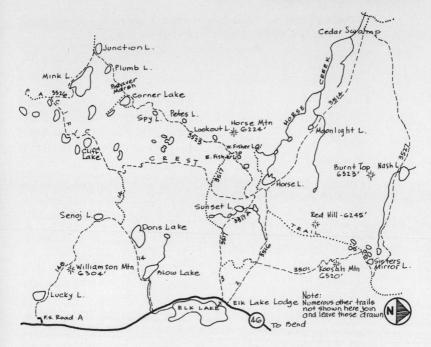

Trail Map for Trips A, B, C, and D

Trip Outlines

Trip A   8 miles, loop hike: overnight or day hike
Start on east side of Wilderness where F.S. Trail 2 leaves
State 46 (4900) at northwest end of Elk Lake. Hike up to
ridge (5300) and F.S. Trail 3501. Take F.S. Trail 3516 to
Horse Lake. Lunch or camp here. 3½ miles.

Return via short portion of Pacific Crest Trail, F.S. Trail
3517A to Sunset Lake, and F.S. Trails 3517 and 3 to State
46 just south of starting point. 4½ miles.

Trip B   24 miles, loop hike: 3 days, 2 nights
Start same as Trip A. Hike to junction of F.S. Trail 3501.
Take this trail to climb Koosah Mountain (6520) and descend to junction of Pacific Crest Trail. To the north a short
distance are Camelot Lake and Sisters Mirror Lake (6000).
Camp here. 6½ miles.

Second Day. Leave Pacific Crest Trail at junction of F.S.
Trail 3527 and hike west, down to Nash Lake and on to junction with F.S. Trail 3514 (4300). Camp here on Horse Creek
or Cedar Swamp. 9 miles.

Third Day. Ascend F.S. Trail 3514. Pass Moonlight Lake
and reach Horse Lake (4930) and junction with Pacific Crest
Trail. Take this east a short way to reach F.S. Trail 3516 and
return to State 46. 8½ miles.

Trip C   28½ miles, loop hike: 4 days, 3 nights
Start as in Trip A. Instead of taking F.S. Trail 3517A, continue on Pacific Crest Trail to junction of F.S. Trail 3523.
Ascend this trail to Platt Lake and East and West Fisher
lakes. Pass east of Horse Mountain (6224). Pass F.S. Trail
3517 and descend into Mink Lake Basin. Pass Lookout
Lake, Pete's Lake, and Spy Lake to reach Cabin Meadows
and Corner Lake (4750). Camp here. 9 miles.

Second Day. Continue on F.S. Trail 3523. Pass Beaver
Marsh and Plumb Lake. Reach Junction Lake (4918) and
junction with trail to Mink Lake (5034). Take F.S. Trail
3526 to Pacific Crest Trail. Take Pacific Crest Trail north to
Cliff Lake. Camp here. 7 miles.

Third Day. Continue on Pacific Crest Trail to Horse Lake
(4930). Camp here. 8½ miles.

Fourth Day. Return to State 46 via F.S. Trails 3516 and 2. 4
miles.

Observations This is very easy going. By adding a day or two to this trip and changing campsites it could become a very pleasant fishing trip.

Trip D 10½ miles, one way: 2 days, 1 night
Start on east side of Wilderness where F.S. Trail 14 leaves State 46 about a half-mile south of Elk Lake (4950). Hike into Blow Lake and Doris Lake. Reach junction with F.S. Trail 14B. Take this trail south to Senoj Lake. Camp here. 4½ miles.

Second Day. Climb to skirt Williamson Mountain (6301) and descend to Lucky Lake and on to F.S. Road A from State 46.

WASHINGTON

Washington is a land of many wilderness areas, forests, and vast national parks set aside for scientific study and recreation. Along the Cascade Mountain Range, running north to south through the state, the volcanic glacier peaks of Glacier Mountain, Mt. Rainier, and Mt. Adams rise impressively above thousands of square miles of snow-capped mountains, great forests, streams and lakes, and remote backcountry.

About 40 million people can reach this land within two days' drive. Interstate highways make traveling easy for people who want to reach such popular places as Olympic and Mt. Rainier national parks, or the lesser known Mt. Adams Wilderness and Mt. Margaret Backcountry.

Miles of trails are maintained in these areas. There are popular day trips to scenic alpine lakes or overnighters and longer trips into remote regions.

Hikers can obtain a very complete set of trail guidebooks and reference material from the Mountaineers, an organization dedicated to the exploration, study, recording, and preservation of the natural wonders in this state. Their books are handsomely printed and complemented by outstanding photographs. For a book list write the Mountaineers, P.O. Box 122, Seattle, Washington 98111.

MOUNT RAINIER NATIONAL PARK

Mount Rainier, 14,410 feet, is a towering landmark in western Washington. This dormant volcano is mantled with the ice of many glaciers nourishing the lower green landscape of dense forests. Volcanic eruptions that started about one million years ago, along with the subsequent action of ice ages and the elements, have shaped Mount Rainier. This process continues. With the approach of summer and warm weather, melting glaciers begin to move as much as 16 inches a day, grinding away parts of the mountain. Summer weather here is mixed, but mainly moderate. Winter storms are severe, with as much as 80 feet of snow falling. At lower elevations snow remains until late July, when the open forests and meadows bloom in a wonderful display of color.

Season The park is open year round. However, most facilities are open only during summer months. Hiking is best from July through September. After July 15 for high trails.

Location The park lies in west-central Washington, southeast of Seattle and Tacoma by a two-hour drive. The Snoqualmie and Gifford Pinchot national forests surround the park.

Access U.S. 12 passes the park's southern border. From this, State 123 goes north into the park. State 410, 7, and 706 lead south to the park from the Seattle-Tacoma area. Interstate 80 and 90 (east-west) and Interstate 5 (north-south) bring traffic to the area.

Transportation Services Private bus service from Tacoma

and Seattle June to mid-September. For rates write Rainier National Park Company, Box 1136, Tacoma, Washington 98401.

Accommodations   Overnight accommodations are found on all the roads leading to the park. Within the park there are inns at Longmire and Paradise. Write address above for season, rates, and reservations. In the park and surrounding it are many campgrounds.

Medical Assistance   Park first aid. Private assistance in Morton.

Fishing   Trout. No license required. Some streams limited to fly fishing only. Check regulations and seasons at park.

Hunting   None.

Recreation   East of the park Puget Sound country awaits the visitor. Seattle and Tacoma offer all the big-city attractions in the way of food, lodgings, and entertainment. Summer travelers in this area will be especially pleased with the fine fresh fruit crops.

Driving all the way to the Pacific Ocean, one can turn north to the unique rain forest of Olympic National Park or south to the historic sites of the Lewis and Clark expedition at the mouth of the Columbia River.

Park Trails   Mount Rainier National Park is 378 square miles in area. Centered in the park is Mount Rainier, occupying one-fourth of the area. Surrounding the mountain, and on its slopes, are over 300 miles of trails.

The trails are generally in good condition. However, winter conditions, floods, avalanches, and lingering snow can either alter or obliterate trails. Be sure to check with park rangers about trail conditions.

Fire permits are required. Camping is at designated areas.

Water is plentiful.

References Write for *A Guide to the Trails of Mt. Rainier National Park,* Mt. Rainier Natural History Association, Longmire, Washington 98397. 75 cents. Also ask for the park brochure.

15 x 25 minute quadrangle: Mt. Rainier National Park, from above address, 80 cents.

Trip Outlines

Trip A 16½ miles, loop hike: 2 days, 1 night
At northwest corner of park start hike at Ipsut Campground (2300), 5 miles east of the Carbon River entrance to the park. Ascend to Mowich Lake along Ipsut Creek. This is a section of the Wonderland Trail. Good water here in this heavy forest. Tall trees are moss-draped and reaching to 250 feet. Mosses and ferns spread over the forest floor. Look for signs noting largest Alaska cedar in the world. Climb steeply to Ipsut Pass (5100) via switchbacks on open trail. Turn right to ascend Tolmie Peak (5939). Take left to reach Mowich Lake (4929). Camp at south end of lake. 5½ miles.

Second Day. Leave Wonderland Trail about ¼ mile south of Mowich Lake and take Spray Park Trail south in the forest to the edge of Eagle Cliff; then climb steeply alongside Hessong Rock to Spray Park and the high country. This is rugged hiking, possibly through snow, but the vistas are magnificent. Late summer brings the wild flowers and birds. Cross over Spray Park (6300) and begin descent of over 3,000 feet. Enter treeline and reach Cataract Creek. Hike down and under Echo Cliffs on right. Reach the Carbon River and the Wonderland Trail. Follow this river trail down to Ipsut Campground. 11 miles.

Trip B 37 miles, loop hike: 4 days, 3 nights
This hike is for those who feel they can make the daily mileage. Start hike as in *Trip A.* Take Wonderland Trail up Carbon River to junction with North Loop Trail to Lake James (2800).

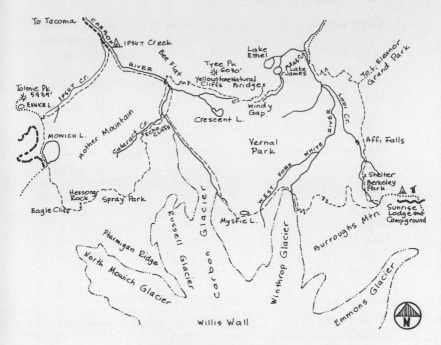

Trail Map for Trips A and B

Easy grade and deep forest to this point. Then start steep climb to Bee Flat (4600). Leave treeline and continue up under Tyee Peak (6030) and Yellowstone Cliffs to the high country. Reach Windy Gap (5700) and great views of Puget Sound country. Spur trail left to Natural Bridge, a great stone arch. Descend to forest and camp at Lake James (4370). 7½ miles.

Second Day. Descend via switchback through forest to cross White River. Then start climbing through open slopes to Grand Park and junction (5700) with trail to Lake Eleanor. Keep right and continue across Grand Park to Affi Falls and up to shelter cabin at Berkeley Park (5700). Camp here. 9½ miles.

Third Day. Ascend from Berkeley Park to junction (6500) of Wonderland Trail coming from Sunrise. Take Wonderland Trail west under Winthrop Glacier to Mystic Lake and shelter (5800). Camp here. 10 miles.

Fourth Day. Continue along Wonderland Trail, descending beside Carbon Glacier through Moraine Park and under the Northern Crags on right. Look back at the towering Willis Wall, 3,600 feet high above the summit of Carbon Glacier. In midsummer ice avalanches thunder down the cliff to feed Carbon Glacier. Reach junction of Spray Park coming from left. Continue ahead and down to Carbon River and Ipsut Campground. 10 miles.

Observation   There is some hard hiking in this trip. The third day well warrants an early start. However, the vistas are matchless, the experience priceless.

Another trip to be made, and a real adventure, might be 10-12 days along the Wonderland Trail (mentioned above). This trail circles Mount Rainier for 90 miles. It passes over, through, and around every conceivable terrain: primeval forests, alpine meadows, glaciers, and streams. There are shelters at the end of each day's hike, and Mount Rainier is ever present.

OLYMPIC NATIONAL PARK

Comprising 897,000 acres, Olympic National Park embraces dense rain forest, mountains, glaciers, lakes, and streams. Its great trees shelter abundant wildlife, and fishing is good. Although there are few roads, the park boasts 600 miles of trails with shelters. Hikers can expect wet weather.

To secure map-brochures, write Olympic National Park, 600 East Park Avenue, Port Angeles, Washington 98362.

NORTH CASCADES NATIONAL PARK

This is one of the nation's new parks, over one thousand square miles of magnificent alpine scenery. Situated as a great preserve extending over the North Cascades Mountain Range, it is a region of jagged peaks, glaciers, lakes, and streams.

The park is in four sections: the North Unit, Ross Lake National Recreation Area, the South Unit, and Lake Chelan National Recreation Area. Pasayten Wilderness is to the east, while Glacier Peaks Wilderness is to the south, comprising a vast area of wild country.

The peaks in this park rise above more than 150 glaciers giving birth to spectacular waterfalls and sparkling streams, sustaining alpine lakes and forested slopes. Western slopes are cloaked with dark rain forests of conifers, green meadows, wild flowers, and alpine tundra. On the eastern slopes are pine forests, broad fields, and scrub growth.

Mountain goats, deer, and black bear are native. The grizzly bear and cougar belong here, too. Bald eagles can be seen feeding on salmon on the Skagit during winter.

Season August and September. Snow can stay on the trails through July and come in October.

Location North Cascades National Park is located in northwestern Washington, less than a three-hour drive from the Seattle-Tacoma area.

Access Presently there is only one way to reach the park by car. From the west take State 20 from Interstate 5 (north-south). State 20 through to the east is under construction at this writing, and is scheduled to be completed by 1973. On the east side of the park there is boat and plane service from Chelan on

U.S. 97 to Stehekin at the north end of Lake Chelan. Interstate 90 (east-west) and U.S. 97 and U.S. 2 bring hikers to this area.

The trail data here is concerned with the western access.

Transportation Services   None.

Accommodations   Motels and lodges along State 20 west of the park. Campgrounds in the park.

Medical Assistance   Sedro Wooley on State 20. Bellingham at west end of State 542.

Fishing   All the trout in the lakes and streams. Washington state license needed. Buy one locally or write Washington Game Department, 600 North Capitol Way, Olympia, Washington 98501.

Hunting   None in the two units of the park. Hunting is allowed in both recreation areas. For seasons, game, licenses, write as above.

Park Trails   There are about 345 miles of trails in this area. At present there are few loop hikes. One-way trips are such that to dead head a car requires a drive of over 150 miles from Diablo Lake (State 20) west, north, and then east to Mt. Baker Lodge on State 542.

Water is plentiful.

A campfire permit is required. Camping is at designated areas only. However, some camps are too far apart for many hikers. Check with rangers for permits, and about routes and alternate campsites for shorter days.

References   Write for map-brochure of the park, North Cascades National Park, Skagit District Headquarters, Marblemount, Washington 98267. Ask for *Main Trails and Back Country Camp Areas,* and a map-brochure of Mount Baker National Forest.

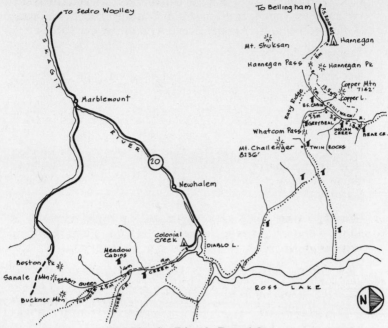

Trail Map for Trips A, B, and C

Trip Outlines

Trip A   28 miles, return trip: 4 days, 3 nights
Take State 20 east into the park to Colonial Creek
Campground. Trail starts at south end of South Unit. Take
easy ascent along Thunder Creek. Pass junction of trail to
Fourth of July Pass on left. Pass Middle Cabin at about 5½
miles. Pass Fisher Creek Crossing. Reach ascent via switch-
backs to camp at junction of Fisher Creek and Thunder
Creek trails. Camp here. 9 miles.

Second Day. Take Thunder Creek Trail and descend into valley. Pass trail to Meadow Cabins on right. Ascend to Skagit Queen Creek draining the Boston Glacier below Boston Peak (8894), Sanale Mountain (8425), and Buckner Mountain. Camp here. 4½ miles.

Third Day. Return to junction of Meadow Cabins Trail. Take trail left to camp at Meadow Cabins. 4½ miles.

Fourth Day. Return to Colonial Creek Campground via first- and second-day route. 10 miles, mostly descending.

Observations   This makes an ideal hike for those who want to spend time birdwatching or fishing on the second and third days.

Trip B   38½ miles, loop hike: 4 days, 3 nights
Base in the northwest corner of the park at Hannegan Campground (3000) at the end of F.S. Road 402, leaving State 542 before reaching Mt. Baker Lodge. With an early morning start, climb to Hannegan Pass (5066) and descend to pass Copper Mountain Trail, Hell's Gorge, and Easy Ridge Trail junction, and reach U.S. Cabin (2600). Camp here. 10 miles.

Second Day. Descend to find Chilliwack River (use caution here during heavy rain or snowmelts; check river condition with rangers when getting a camping permit). Pass Whatcom Pass Trail junction, Indian Creek Shelter, and Copper Mountain Trail to the left, and reach Bear Creek Shelter. Camp here. 8½ miles.

Third Day. Retrace steps to Copper Mountain Trail on right. Ascend to Copper Lake (6133). This is a stiff climb. Camp at lake. 9 miles.

Fourth Day. Hike to Copper Mountain, Egg Lake, and Hannegan Pass (5066). Descend to Hannegan Campground and parked car. 11 miles.

Observations This is hard hiking, terrain and mileage. Add another day to the trip and camp at sites of your choice after getting permission from the park rangers.

Trip C 48 miles, return trip: 5 days, 4 nights
Start as in Trip B: first day is the same 10 miles.

Second Day. Proceed as in Trip B until reaching the Whatcom Pass Trail junction on right. Ascend to Whatcom Pass (5206). Mt. Challenger is on right. Descend to Twin Rocks Shelter. Camp here. 9 miles.

Third Day. Return over Whatcom Pass and descend to meet Chilliwack Trail. Turn right and hike to Indian Creek Shelter. Camp here. About 9½ miles.

Fourth Day. Continue on to junction of Copper Mountain Way Trail on left. Ascend about 3,000 feet out of Chilliwack Drainage and hike ridge to Copper Lake (6133). Camp here. 8½ miles.

Fifth Day. Same as fourth day of Trip B. 11 miles.

Observations This is not a hike to make unless the morning starts are early. If another day were added and other camp-sites used, this could be a very leisurely 8 miles a day.

GOAT ROCKS WILDERNESS

Bands of mountain goats inhabit this mountainous, 82,670-acre preserve. While not an area of high peaks (only Mt. Curtis Gilbert rises above 8,000 feet), it is nevertheless a craggy, al-pine wilderness with much of its terrain above timberline.

The Goat Rocks are part of the Volcanic Cascades, rocky pinnacles rising above snowfields and glaciers. From its high trails one can see Mt. Adams and the impressive Mt. Rainier.

This is an area of few lakes, but many glacier-fed streams cascade down rocky slopes into forest and meadows ablaze with colorful wild flowers in July and August. Surrounding forests are mostly coniferous, becoming weather-worn and stunted at higher altitudes.

Aside from mountain goats grazing in the upper meadows, there are elk and deer. Bear, coyote, and the occasional cougar frequent the area.

Season   July 15 through September. After August 1 to be sure the high trails are free of snow.

Location   The Goat Rocks Wilderness is in southern Washington astride the Cascade Mountain Range. Mt. Rainier National Park is to the north. The wilderness lies within the Gifford Pinchot and Snoqualmie national forests.

Access   This area is a short drive from Seattle-Tacoma, Yakima, and Portland, Oregon. U.S. 12 (east-west) passes the north border. Interstate 5 (north-south) and Interstates 80 and 90 (east-west) bring traffic to the area.

Transportation Services   None.

Accommodations   Motels and lodges along U.S. 12. Campgrounds along U.S. 12 and on the F.S. roads leading to the area's west border.

Medical Assistance   Morton on U.S. 12.

Fishing   Cutthroat, rainbow, and eastern brook trout in the streams and lakes. Buy a license locally or write Washington Game Department, 600 North Capitol Way, Olympia, Washington 98501.

Hunting   For seasons, game, and licenses, write same as above.

Wilderness Trails   About 100 miles of trails will help the backpacker reach this magnificent alpine scenery. The Pacific Crest Trail is the main link in this system of trails, winding its way along the ridges and peaks for 42 miles. This is an area suited to day trips or overnighters.

The trails are in good condition. Trail heads and junctions are signed.

Water is plentiful.

Fire permits are not required. There are enough campsites here to use one of the designated areas.

References Write for map-brochure, *Goat Rocks Wilderness,* District Ranger, Packwood Ranger Station, Packwood, Washington 98361. This is an excellent colored topo map with all the trails. Also ask for map-brochure of the Gifford Pinchot National Forest.

Trip Outlines

Trip A   12 miles, return trip: 2 days, 1 night
On U.S. 12 just east of White Pass, opposite the entrance to White Pass Campground, take Pacific Crest Trail south to ascend steeply via switchbacks to Ginette Lake (5400). Pass F.S. Trail 1144 from left leading to Twin Peaks and Round Mountain. Continue ahead with easy ascent to reach Goat Rocks Wilderness Boundary. Pass Trail to White Pass Ski Area on right and reach Hogback Mountain. Trail is at about 6,400 feet. Miriam Lake on left below. Excellent views of Goat Rocks and country surrounding. Continue on to Shoe Lake (5800). Camp here. 6 miles.

Second Day. Return to U.S. 12.

An alternate here would be to consider this as a day trip. Take a lunch to eat somewhere on Hogback Mountain. About 9 miles, return trip.

Trip B   15 miles, loop hike: 2 days, 1 night
From U.S. 12, about 3 miles west of Packwood, take F.S. Road 1302 to Chambers Lake and Berry Patch parking lot (4800). Take F.S. Trail 95 to junction with F.S. Trail 96.

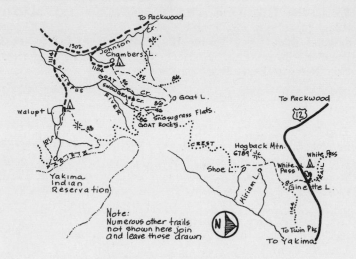

Trail Map for Trips A, B, and C

Take this trail along mountainside. Reach Goat Creek and camping spot. Cross creek and begin steep ascent to Snowgrass Creek (5500). Pass cutoff trail to Pacific Crest Trail. Pass F.S. Trail 86 to Pacific Crest Trail. Reach junction: F.S. Trail 86 to left and F.S. Trail 96 to right. Turn right and climb to Pacific Crest Trail and Snowgrass Flats (6400).

At 4 miles this makes a good lunch stop or the turning point for a day hike.

Continue north along Pacific Crest Trail to Old Snowy Mountain (7930). View the glaciers and Goat Rocks. Later in the afternoon retrace steps to junction with F.S. Trail 96. Descend to junction of F.S. Trail 86. Turn north to Alpine Camp. Camp here. About 8 miles.

Second Day. Hike north on F.S. Trail 86 to Goat Lake (6400). Reach junction of F.S. Trail 95 and 90. Take F.S. Trail 95 and descend into Upper Jordan Basin. Pass Bluff Camp. Pass Buckhorn Camp. Pass F.S. Trail 94 to right and descend from Goat Ridge to Berry Patch parking lot. 8 miles.

Observations   This trip has easy ascents and matchless scenery.

Trip C   14 miles, loop hike: 2 days, 1 night
From U.S. 12 about 3 miles south of Packwood take F.S. Road 1302 and 1114 to Walupt Lake (3927). Start hike at east end of Walupt Lake Campground. Take F.S. Trail 101 around north shore of lake. Reach Walupt Creek. Ascend via switchbacks to reach Pacific Crest Trail. Some small ponds and lakes here. Good lunch stop. Continue north on Pacific Crest Trail. To the right is Yakima Indian Reservation. Reach junction of F.S. Trail 98 from Walupt Lake. Turn south along F.S. Trail 98 to camp. 8 miles.

Second Day. Continue on F.S. Trail 98 along ridge and descend via switchbacks to start of hike. 6 miles.

Deadend Trail in Cranberry Backcountry

INDEX